Better Homes and Gardens.

decorative PAINTING MADE EASY

Better Homes and Gardens. Books
Des Moines, Iowa

Better Homes and Gardens® Books
An imprint of Meredith® Books

Decorative Painting Made Easy
Editor: Amy Tincher-Durik
Senior Associate Design Director: John Eric Seid
Decorative Painter: Patty Mohr Kramer
Contributing Stylist: Cathy Kramer, Cathy Kramer Designs
Contributing Photographer: Kent Clawson
Copy Chief: Terri Fredrickson
Copy and Production Editor: Victoria Forlini
Editorial Operations Manager: Karen Schirm
Managers, Book Production: Pam Kvitne, Marjorie J. Schenkelberg, Rick von Holdt
Contributing Copy Editor: Ro Sila
Contributing Proofreaders: Kathi DiNicola, Sue Fetters, Vivian Mason
Illustrator: Jim Swanson
Indexer: Kathleen Poole
Electronic Production Coordinator: Paula Forest
Editorial and Design Assistants: Kaye Chabot, Karen McFadden, Mary Lee Gavin

Meredith® Books
Editor in Chief: Linda Raglan Cunningham
Design Director: Matt Strelecki
Executive Editor, Home Decorating and Design: Denise L. Caringer

Publisher: James D. Blume
Executive Director, Marketing: Jeffrey Myers
Executive Director, New Business Development: Todd M. Davis
Executive Director, Sales: Ken Zagor
Director, Operations: George A. Susral
Director, Production: Douglas M. Johnston
Business Director: Jim Leonard

Vice President and General Manager: Douglas J. Guendel

Better Homes and Gardens® Magazine
Editor in Chief: Karol DeWulf Nickell

Meredith Publishing Group
President, Publishing Group: Stephen M. Lacy
Vice President-Publishing Director: Bob Mate

Meredith Corporation
Chairman and Chief Executive Officer: William T. Kerr

Chairman of the Executive Committee: E. T. Meredith III

All of us at Better Homes and Gardens® Books are dedicated to providing you with
information and ideas to enhance your home. We welcome your comments and
suggestions. Write to us at: Better Homes and Gardens Books, Home Decorating and
Design Editorial Department, 1716 Locust St., Des Moines, IA 50309-3023.

If you would like to purchase any of our home decorating and design, cooking, crafts,
gardening, or home improvement books, check wherever quality books are sold. Or visit
us at: bhgbooks.com

Cover Photograph: Hopkins Associates

TABLE OF CONTENTS

Introduction, page 4

This comprehensive section includes everything you need to know about selecting the right colors and decorative painting techniques to add personality to your living spaces.

Section One: Create Texture with Glazes, page 26

In this section you will learn about the magic of glazes. When mixed with paint and applied—or removed—with sponges, rags, notched combs, and even common plastic wrap, glaze has the ability to create a wide range of visual textures.

Section Two: All in Good Measure, page 84

With a little planning, you can design an exciting array of geometric designs—let this section show you how. The best part? You can incorporate nearly any of the techniques in Sections One and Three to make your design truly one of a kind.

Section Three: Techniques with Specialty Tools, page 116

This diverse collection of techniques is sure to jumpstart your creativity. You'll be amazed at the exciting looks you can create with everything from diluted paint applied to unfinished wood to wallpaper that resembles a faux paint finish when torn and adhered to a project surface.

Credits and Resources, page 188

Look here to find many of the paint colors and products featured in this book—as well as where to purchase them.

Index, page 192

This easy-to-use resource will help you navigate throughout this book.

Technique Glossary, page 193

Tear this special section out of the book and voila: You have an instant opportunity to audition 15 of the techniques featured in this book. Each technique is shown full-size and in two color combinations so you'll know exactly how the technique will look on your wall or other project surface before committing time and energy.

INTRODUCTION: Part One

I'LL NEVER FORGET THE DAY my parents allowed me to choose new paint, wallpaper, and accessories for my bedroom. I was 9 years old, and I still remember the excitement of selecting paint chips and thumbing through wallpaper books. As a child, selecting the color for my room was easy: I just chose my favorite color, purple, and based all my decisions around that.

When my husband and I were faced with selecting colors for an entire house many years later, I realized something changed. No longer was I thinking about one small 10×10 space; I was suddenly confronted with finding colors that worked together to unify all the rooms in our home. I also realized that selecting colors isn't the only consideration when painting the interiors of a house. Using the right tools with correct techniques is just as important.

We made quite a few mistakes in that first house—and I'm sure the masking tape we used to mask off moldings and window frames is still stuck in some places—but through trial and error and a few color mishaps, we became more confident about our ability to choose the right colors and decorative painting techniques to enhance our home and smarter about how we approached each painting project. I created this book—which is filled with tried-and-true painting and color selection methods and more than 25 exciting techniques—to serve as a roadmap for you as you begin your next painting adventure.

HOW TO USE THIS BOOK

Before you choose a technique and jump right into any project—even if you are eager to make your mark on a sea of white walls—review Choosing Colors with Confidence, beginning on page 6. This will give you the basic information you need to help you choose a color scheme for any room. And, even if you have painted before, review the essentials of painting, Before You Paint, starting on page 16. The foolproof techniques will ensure painting success—and you'll learn about everything from the difference between latex and alkyd paint to how to choose the right roller.

When you are ready to begin painting, select a technique that best suits your skill level and the look you desire, using the Technique Glossary beginning on page 193. This special section showcases 15 of the techniques in various color combinations. The best part? The samples are full size and can be separated from the book, so you can hold the samples up to your wall or other surface to envision how the final painted technique will look.

The 27 techniques range in difficulty from easy colorwashing that can be achieved in an afternoon to more advanced marbling that requires patience and practice to master. As you peruse this book, keep in mind that nearly all of the techniques are suitable for more than just walls: Floors, ceilings, and even that unfinished bookshelf in the corner are prime surfaces on which to let your personality shine.

Section One covers the exciting world of glazes. When mixed with any color of paint, glaze—paint without pigment—allows you to create an astonishing array of visual textures on a surface. Whether you love the coarse weave of crisp linen or long for walls that are delicately sponged, this section will show you real-world examples of rooms sure to jumpstart your creativity.

If bold geometric patterns, from wide playful stripes to romantic harlequin diamonds, inspire you to grab a paintbrush, but you aren't sure where to begin, fear not. Section Two is designed to help you take the guesswork out of planning and executing geometric patterns of any scale.

While nearly every technique featured in the first two sections of this book uses a special tool or material—for instance a sea sponge, a check roller, or common household plastic wrap—the techniques featured in Section Three incorporate everything from feathers to sandpaper to achieve a unique look. This collection even features techniques such as decoupage that can be combined with paint for a wide array of effects and wallpaper that looks like a faux paint technique when torn and applied to a surface.

Regardless of whether you have picked up this book to glean information on selecting colors or you are ready to devote a weekend to painting your bedroom, relax. Have fun. Experiment. Let go and allow the blank surfaces in your home to become a canvas where you can be free to express yourself with color, pattern, and visual texture; when you give yourself permission to do so, you may wonder why you didn't do it sooner.

Amy Tincher-Durik

Amy Tincher-Durik
Editor, Decorative Painting Made Easy

tips ideas color

tools walls floors ceilings

furniture glazes textures

how-to patterns finishes special effects

Choosing Colors with Confidence

WHEN MOST PEOPLE ARE READY TO FRESHEN AND PERSONALIZE THEIR LIVING SPACES—or when they move into a new home—one of the very first things they think about is color, namely paint. To help you take the guesswork out of choosing color for your next painting adventure, this section has been developed to take you through the selection process.

▲ This entryway and living area prove that mixing and matching colors can be very invigorating. The space features a blend of warm (orange and yellow) and cool (purple) for an exciting color scheme.

Don't fret if the array of paint brands, finishes, and color chips is overwhelming, or you aren't sure what technique suits your decorating style. **That's what this book is all about: Giving you the confidence to choose the colors and techniques that will let your personality shine in your home.**

GETTING STARTED

BEFORE YOU BEGIN CHOOSING COLORS FOR A PARTICULAR ROOM, think about the following: What sort of mood do you want the space to create? A serene, restful retreat or an invigorating, lively space? How is the room used? Is this space your private hideaway or is it a high-traffic, high-energy area? What colors do you—and your family—love? Soft pastels, bold jewel tones, or earthy neutrals? What items, including furnishings, window treatments, and artwork, will be in the room? By considering these questions you are on the right track for choosing the right colors for your home and the way you live.

To help you consider the mood of a space, and which colors and techniques work well with a particular decorating style, see the Technique Primer on page 24. See pages 10 to 13 for information on colors and their characteristics. Remember that this information is a guide; it's your home, you have to live with it, and if it doesn't appeal to the neighbors does it really matter? If you and your family love bright primary colors, go for it!

By working around what you have, you've begun with a roadmap to follow. In fact relying on furnishings and accessories you already have and love is a great way to choose a paint color. If you are starting with a blank slate, however, select items you like that will likely be housed in the room, like an upholstered chair or painting, and build from there. The trick, however, is to pair paint colors with these items but not match them exactly; replicating a decoration in a wall color might detract from it, causing it to take a backseat or even fade into the walls.

When you go to a paint store or home improvement center to select paint colors, take a swatch of fabric, a sample of carpet, or even the piece of art to help with the process. If you can't find an exact match and desire one, the sample may be placed in a device called a spectrophotometer that will read the color and formulate a recipe of pigments that matches the sample. Gather a good sampling of chips—choose neighboring chips, or those that are above, below, and beside the one you prefer—and take them home to get a better sense of how they will work there. Once at home you can start eliminating any chips that don't appeal to you. Use the guidelines right and on page 8 to help you understand how colors are affected by such factors as light, finish, and wall texture and how to use the paint chips and cards you have gathered to make your final choice.

colors and the environment

Selecting the right color or colors for your space is much easier when you keep the following principles in mind:

❶ drying time changes color: Paint usually dries darker than it appears when wet. For a more accurate view of what the color will look like, paint a sample board of the same texture as your wall.

❷ light changes color: Move the sample board around the room, observing how it appears near natural and artificial light, as well as in the morning and evening.

❸ sheen changes color: A flat, matte paint differs in look from the same color in a shiny, glossy finish. The shinier the color the lighter it will look.

❹ texture affects color: Smooth surfaces reflect light, so a heavily textured wall will appear darker than a smooth wall that's the same color.

❺ colors affect one another: Move the sample board around the room, close to various furnishings or other elements to see how it will "fit" in the room.

▼ When choosing colors for a room, it is easiest to use what you have—flooring, rugs, and furniture upholstery—for color cues rather than starting with a wall color and decorating around it.

◀ Use the things you love, such as artwork, as a starting point for choosing color.

using paint chips and cards

Paint chips and cards found at paint stores and home improvement centers are great tools for selecting colors, but understanding how to use them is the first step in developing a successful color scheme.

■ On many paint cards a portion of a single color family is represented in graduated sequence, with only subtle differences between the adjacent chips.

■ To get a true idea of what the real hue will look like on your wall, cut away the white spaces on the paint card. Then check the color against those colors with which it will be used for an accurate representation.

■ The small size of color chips makes it difficult to envision how that color will look on a large wall. What looks appropriate on the small card may appear quite different on a wall. To get a better idea of how your color will really look, cover the surrounding chips on the card with your fingers, hold the chip against the wall, and squint.

▶ Nature provides a delightful resource for observing and selecting colors for your spaces.

the color wheel

THE COLOR WHEEL is divided into cool colors (between yellow-green and violet) and warm colors (between yellow and red-violet). Cool colors impart a restful atmosphere, whereas warm colors are action colors that make a room seem lively and happy. The variations within each of these colors lie in value and tone, which change the way a color appears (see below for definitions).

This basic understanding of color will help you choose the best colors for your particular project. While you can certainly select what you like and paint away, taking the entire room and its contents into consideration—and how they affect one another—is important, as outlined on page 7. If you are feeling a bit timid about pulling a color scheme together, don't worry: The following pages present some guidelines to assist with the process, including the basic characteristics of cool, warm, and neutral

colors, how color visually affects a space, and choosing a whole-house color scheme. Keep in mind that often the most successful color schemes include a mix of cool and warm colors: Cool colors often require a warm-up from invigorating colors, while warm colors need a splash of calm to cool them down.

In a color scheme, the dominant color inhabits the greatest amount of space in a room. This dominant color can be the walls, ceilings, or even a portion of the floor. The secondary color is the color that has the next "level of importance" in the room. Often it is brighter than the dominant color. Subordinate colors are often less lively and should be used for items that you want to blend into the background, while accent colors are the splashes of color that enliven a room. Accent colors are often selected from the opposite side of the color wheel from the dominant color.

COOL COLORS

WARM COLORS

---

color terms and schemes defined

HUE: Term often used interchangeably with color.

VALUE: This is how light or dark a color is. A tint (mixed with white) of a color has a light value, while a shade (mixed with black) of a color has a dark value.

TONE: A color or hue mixed with black and white.

PRIMARY COLORS: These are the pure colors—red, blue, and yellow—that cannot be made by mixing other colors. All other colors are made by mixing parts of these colors together.

SECONDARY COLORS: These colors are created when equal parts of two primary colors are mixed together: Red and yellow create orange; red and blue create purple; and blue and yellow create green.

COMPLEMENTARY COLORS: These colors are opposite each other on the color wheel, so both a warm and a cool color are represented. Pairing the two

creates more energy than either color would have alone, but it is wise to let one color dominate so the two don't compete.

COOL COLORS: These colors relax spaces and appear to recede. Cool schemes need a jolt of warm color to enliven them.

WARM COLORS: These colors invigorate spaces and appear to advance. Warm schemes need a touch of a cool hue for balance.

ANALOGOUS SCHEME: Colors that lie next to each other on the color wheel are analogous. Because these colors share a common hue they work well together.

MONOCHROMATIC SCHEME: In a monochromatic scheme all of the elements are dominated by one color. Incorporating patterns and values rather than solid colors as accents makes a monochromatic scheme work.

all about COOL colors

THE COOL COLORS ARE BLUE, GREEN, AND PURPLE (VIOLET). These colors are often more restful than the sunny warm colors, but different levels of intensity can greatly alter how a cool color appears.

blue, the color of calm, is the color equivalent of aromatherapy: It encourages you to slow your pace and breathe deeply. Note that while blue is tranquil, a room painted entirely in pastel blue may appear chilly. To warm a blue-dominated space, incorporate neutral or warm accents in the furnishings. Dark blue can add quiet drama to spaces, while warmer blues, such as periwinkle, promote calm in rooms where people tend to gather.

purple is traditionally considered a regal color, but it can take on different personalities depending on its hue and whether the red (warm) or blue (cool) is dominant. In dark values such as eggplant purple appears sophisticated, and in light values like lilac it is restful.

green is a versatile color: It is the combination of refreshing blue and cheery yellow, so it can work in multiple decorating schemes. True green is springlike and fresh, while grayed greens are subtle enough to mix with any other color.

A vivid shade of GREEN for the walls, YELLOW cabinets, and RED accents bring an exciting burst of color to this kitchen. The green adds cool contrast to the space, keeping the warm colors from overpowering it.

White woodwork graphically outlines the PURPLE and GREEN walls in this dining room.

Two shades of BLUE paint seem to make the walls of this bedroom extend into the heavens. The blues are calm and serene.

all about WARM colors

SUNNY, TANGY REDS, YELLOWS, AND ORANGES ARE THE PERFECT COLORS to bring happiness and the warmth of the sun to any living space. Because they're intense these colors are great for north- and east-facing rooms.

Eye-catching and energizing, **red** is the most intense color of all. This versatile color changes, depending on whether it is used as an accent color or part of a monochromatic scheme. When it appears in an otherwise neutral room, it acts as a lively friend who brightens a gray day. In a living or dining room, red stimulates conversation and the appetite, and it makes a strong first impression in an entryway (see page 15 for an example).

yellow is a unique color in that it has a look for everyone, from its light and cheerful shades of lemon and buttercup to grayed shades of antique gold and caramel. In general, yellow is a great choice for expanding small, dark spaces. "Antiqued" yellows are perfect for period decorating schemes, while grayed yellows are wonderful for traditionally decorated spaces.

orange is the ultimate outgoing color, but like the other colors, it has a versatility that makes it appealing to everyone. This vibrant color ranges from dark tones of warm browns, medium hues of pumpkin and terra-cotta, and light shades of peach, and even aged shades of wicker.

A bright RED wall is sure to bring excitement to any space, especially dining areas: It increases appetite and heightens the sense of taste and smell. The cool blue artwork is a refreshing focal point.

Sunny YELLOW walls paired with crisp white molding create a cheerful environment in which to dine. The yellow visually expands the wide, open space even more.

The artwork on these bright lemon YELLOW and tangy ORANGE walls is the focal point. The wall colors harmonize with rather than detract from the bright, whimsical pieces that incorporate a mix of warm and cool colors.

Choosing Colors with Confidence (continued)

all about NEUTRAL colors

This grouping of colors—black, gray, white, and brown—works well in any color scheme. In small doses, the neutrals blend into the background, allowing the colors to take center stage, but they also have the ability to temper dominant hues, calming things down. To give a neutral scheme visual interest, layer on textures, such as wood furniture, rustic baskets, and woven linens.

When paired with companion neutrals white and brown, BLACK makes a very inviting space. The white pillar and window molding visually break up the black wall, while the white ceiling and light-stained flooring keep things light.

▲ Neutral colors can be used successfully in nearly any decorating style. This dining room has an air of sophistication because it is built around different neutrals, including DARK and LIGHT BROWN, and paired with warm woods.

how color affects SPACE

ONE OF THE MOST EXCITING THINGS ABOUT COLOR is its ability to visually change a space, making it appear taller, shorter, larger, smaller, narrower, wider, further away, or closer. Follow these cues to change the proportions—visually, that is—of any space.

closer: Warm colors advance, making walls seem closer.

narrower: White or light painted ceilings make a room look narrower and taller when paired with dark walls.

larger: Light-color walls cause a room to look larger because they reflect a great deal of light.

shorter: Dark painted ceilings visually make a room appear shorter.

smaller: Walls in dark colors make a room appear smaller because they absorb light rather than reflect it.

taller: White ceilings appear higher.

wider: If you desire a wider-looking room, combine a dark ceiling with light walls.

The long row of white cabinets paired with one BRIGHT YELLOW-ORANGE wall makes this hallway appear shorter.

Light walls, as in this bedroom, make the room appear larger. The WHITE ceiling visually heightens the space.

The combination of DARK WALLS and a DARK CEILING makes this space feel small and cozy.

SMOOTH TRANSITIONS

WHEN UNDERTAKING ANY PAINTING PROJECT, decorative or "plain," it is important to think about how that newly painted space will interact with others in your home. It is likely that some rooms in your home can be seen from other rooms, whether through a doorway or as a result of an open floor plan. Think about how colors flow from room to room and how the colors you select fit into your home's overall interior design.

Even if you can't see multiple rooms from one vantage point, you'll want to ensure the colors and techniques work together to create a sense of cohesiveness throughout your home. That's not to say you can't be daring and try a wildly different treatment in a child's room or bath, but select furnishings and accessories that relate to those throughout the house and consider painting the hallway or area around that room in a way that links it to others.

Strié, or dragging, is effective in traditional settings, as in this dining room, especially when created in deep colors like dark green, royal blue, and rich red. The solid sunny yellow in the adjoining foyer and living room beyond is the perfect complement: It provides a neutral backdrop that emphasizes the strié and holds its own against the classic furnishings.

▲ Soft green and blue easily flow into one another in this open kitchen, dining room, and living room space. The calming colors are found together throughout the space, from the checkerboard tile floor and stained-glass windows to the living room furnishings. Crisp white cabinets and molding provide a clean break between the dining area and living room.

▲ An easy transition from a long hallway to a small foyer results from a well-thought out paint scheme. Bright white combines with lively red throughout most of the space—with one aqua wall thrown in for a splash of cool contrast. The red beneath the chair rail adds visual punch—and keeps the "weight" down, along with the red rug—while the white walls and ceiling make the hallway appear spacious and emphasize the red wall in the foyer that surrounds the door. Red advances, visually shortening the long hallway.

tips for successful transitions

1 NOT ALL WALLS CAN BE FOCAL POINTS. To keep from becoming overwhelmed, it is important to balance decorative techniques with plain, solid painted spaces throughout your home. These neutral spaces will emphasize the decoratively painted areas—and give the eye a rest.

2 CONSIDER HOW DECORATIVE FINISHES COMPLEMENT EACH OTHER, especially when they are in adjoining spaces: A room with a distinctive crackle finish might look awkward when seen from a room with a highly textured denim treatment.

3 THINK ABOUT A WHOLE-HOUSE PALETTE to bring harmony to your home. This can be achieved by choosing one color that appears in every room, for instance painted molding and door frames, repeating color in furnishings and accessories throughout the home, or limiting the overall palette to two or three colors and using them in different doses to add interest to the spaces.

Before You Paint

BEFORE YOU PICK UP A BRUSH OR SELECT ANY OF THE TECHNIQUES IN THIS BOOK, review the information in this section—even if you've painted before. It doesn't hurt to brush up on the basics of preparing a room for painting, the act of painting, and even cleanup—not to mention what paints to choose for your particular project.

ROOM PREPARATION

FIRST THINGS FIRST: Although getting a room ready to paint may take time and energy, don't skip this important step. The work you do to prepare a room correctly prior to painting will be well worth it. To start with, remove anything from the room that is breakable, including small items like knickknacks, and move all furnishings to the center of the room. Cover the furnishings with drop cloths to protect them from paint splatters. Also cover the floors with drop cloths. Remove all outlet and switchplate covers, as well as anything else attached to the walls. To avoid losing the screws that accompany the outlet and switchplate covers, tape them to the backs of the covers.

Unless you are painting on new walls, you may need to smooth out any blemishes with 80-grit sandpaper—or fill in any imperfections with surface compound (see below for more information). Once the compound is dry, sand it smooth. Once you have finished sanding, sweep or vacuum any lingering dust to prevent it from sticking to the wet paint. Wipe down all moldings, including baseboards and casings, with a lint-free cloth to remove dust and debris.

wall repair

To ensure the time and effort you have spent painting will pay off in years to come—or as long as you want the color or technique to stay—it is very important to repair any dents, cracks, or peeling spots on your walls before you paint them. This will give you a smooth surface on which to paint, resulting in an even application. Regardless of which type of repair you have to make, make sure you prime the area prior to painting.

cracks: To patch plaster cracks, first undercut wide cracks to make them broader at the bottom; this helps lock in the filler materials. Blow out any loose plaster. Wet the crack with a sponge, then pack compound into it with a putty knife. Use patching plaster to fill any large holes and cracks. After 24 hours, wet the area again with a sponge and level off with a second coat of patching material. When dry, sand and prime.

dents: To fill dents in drywall, clean any debris out of the depression and sand lightly to roughen the surface. Pack the dent with surface or joint compound; use surface compound for large dents because it shrinks less. For deep depressions and holes, affix fiberglass tape to the damaged area before applying the compound. Let the patch dry overnight, then sand with 150-grit sandpaper or smooth by wiping with a damp sponge. Prime.

flaking or peeled spots: If there are flaky, peeling spots on your walls, oil-base paint that turned brittle over time could be the culprit—or the original surface may not have been properly dulled or cleaned, causing poor paint adhesion. Scrape off loose paint, then sand. Clean interior surfaces with water and a mild household detergent; rinse. Fill any gaps or holes with filler or caulk. Prime. Paint that is older than 20 years may contain lead. If you suspect the old paint contains lead, never sand it and try not to disturb it. Contact a local retailer about how to proceed.

wallpaper: While you can successfully paint over wallpapered walls (see page 22 for more information), it is usually best to remove wallpaper before painting. There are many excellent wallpaper strippers in gel and liquid forms available at hardware and home improvement centers. Follow the manufacturer's instructions for the product you have chosen. For a natural solution, mix 1 part vinegar to 1 part water. Put in a spray bottle and spray onto the wallpaper; peel or scrape away as with commercial products.

◀ A wide range of low-tack painter's tape is available to help ensure crisp, clean lines when painting around moldings and trim. The techniques featured in Section Two, such as stripes and diamonds, utilize painter's tape. See information starting on page 88.

Apply painter's tape, a low-tack quick-release tape, to all moldings and trim to protect these surfaces from paint and to ensure there won't be any gap between the painted wall and molding, revealing the base wall color. While painter's tape is more expensive than regular masking tape, it won't leave a sticky residue on the molding surface. If desired you can also tape drop cloths to the wall to help protect the floor.

THE TOOLS

THE TECHNIQUES PRESENTED IN THIS BOOK REQUIRE THE USE OF NUMEROUS TYPES OF TOOLS, from inexpensive nylon-bristle brushes to specialty weaver brushes and check rollers. For basic painting, however, all you need are good-quality synthetic- or nylon-bristle brushes with flat and angled bristles, a roller and roller cover, and a paint tray. To find out more about the specialty tools and materials needed for a particular technique, see that technique for more information.

When shopping for paintbrushes, choose quality brushes. While they may cost a bit more, they are more durable, and you will be more pleased with the results of your labor. What makes a quality brush? If more than two bristles come out when you tug, it is poorly constructed. Look for a brush with flagged bristles (that look like split ends of hair) that hold more paint, and a sturdy noncorrosive terrule (the metal band wrapped around the bristles and handle). A quality brush measures half again as long as its width: A 2-inch-wide brush should have 3-inch-

▲ Choose a variety of quality paintbrushes for your projects. Flat brushes work for general painting, while angle-bristle, or tapered, brushes are great for trim work. Store brushes in their original, protective plastic covers to help the bristles maintain their shape.

long bristles. Also find a brush that is comfortable to hold.

Buy a variety of brushes ranging from 4 inches wide for walls and ceilings to 1 inch wide for mullions, although a 1½-inch and a 2½-inch brush are appropriate for most painting jobs. Tapered, or angled, brushes are perfect for painting narrow areas of windows, doors, and molding. The shaped bristles allow you to paint clean edges against trim. These brushes have long, thin handles that you hold like a pencil.

Use only synthetic-bristle brushes with latex paint. Natural-hair bristles will frizz if exposed to the water in the paint. You can use natural- or synthetic-bristle brushes with alkyd paint, although natural bristles provide a better finish.

Use short-nap rollers for smooth surfaces and long-nap rollers for rough surfaces. To test the quality of your chosen roller cover, squeeze it. A quality roller will quickly return to its original shape. If you separate the nap on the roller cover you shouldn't be able to see its cardboard core (if you do, it might not be dense enough to deliver a smooth coat of paint). Also, like brushes, use synthetic rollers for water-base and synthetic or natural-fiber rollers for oil-base paint.

▼ Rollers and roller covers come in different sizes to tackle projects of various sizes. When selecting a roller cover, think about the surface you'll be painting: A short-nap roller works best on smooth surfaces, while long-nap rollers are perfect for rough surfaces.

ALL ABOUT PAINTS

WHEN PURCHASING PAINTS, YOU WILL BE FACED WITH NUMEROUS BRANDS AT VARIOUS PRICES. Think quality: Premium paints contain more paint solids (pigments and binders) and less liquid. They are more durable, adhesive, fade-resistant, and uniform in color and sheen—and often require fewer coats for complete coverage. Premium paints are a better long-term investment because they generally require repainting in 10 years instead of the 4 years with less expensive paint.

When you browse the paint aisle at a paint, hardware, or home improvement store, in addition to various brands, you will no doubt see both latex and alkyd paints. All of the techniques featured in this book use latex, or water-base, paints. These paints are safer to use than alkyd, or oil-base, paints and cleanup is a snap with water and mild soap. Regardless, oil-base paints have advantages over latex in some circumstances. Read this section carefully before choosing paints for any project.

Low-odor, fast-drying latex paints have a water base (quality paints have no more than 50 percent water content) and account for the majority of paint sold. Compared with alkyd paints, the color in latex paint is less likely to fade, chalk, crack, or grow mildew. Recent technological advances have made latex paints as adhesive as and longer lasting than oil-base paints; they will resist cracking and chipping better than alkyd paints. Besides general interior painting, latex is the best choice for exterior wood, new stucco, and masonry, or weathered aluminum and vinyl siding.

Alkyd paints are made of petroleum distillates, pigments, and resins; most of the liquid portion is petroleum solvent. The best paints have no more than 30 percent solvent. Oil-base paints are often more durable than latex paints but they are more difficult to use. Oil-base paint has excellent adhesion and fair durability, but it's more likely to harden, become brittle, and yellow over time. It has a strong odor, must be cleaned with

primer

Whether the room you are painting has never been painted or you are painting over a wall that has already been painted, consider using primer prior to repainting. Here are some tips to keep in mind:

✳ Primer is only necessary on new or weathered wood or other raw surfaces, on an uneven or deteriorated painted surface, or on a stripped surface.

✳ Primers and sealers come in latex and alkyd; your primer and paint should always have the same base.

✳ Some primers are formulated for special circumstances, such as stain-blocking primer, drywall primers, and metal primers.

✳ If there are ink and crayon marks or water stains on the surfaces to be painted, use a stain-blocking primer on the walls prior to painting. This will prevent marks and stains from bleeding through the finished paint.

✳ For more complete coverage have primer tinted the same color as the paint over which it will be painted.

mineral spirits or other solvents, including paint thinner, and its drying time is long (from 8 to 24 hours). Alkyd paint is your best choice for exterior surfaces with heavy chalking or when you repaint a surface with four or more layers of old oil-base paint. Do not use oil-base paint on fresh masonry or galvanized iron because the paint will fail quickly.

You can paint latex over oil-base paint, although you must use an oil-base topcoat if you are painting over four or more layers of old oil-base paint. Avoid painting oil-base over latex because the latex underneath is flexible and will expand and contract, causing an oil-base topcoat to crack. To test which paint you have, rub mineral spirits on the surface; oil-base will generally dissolve, whereas latex will be unaffected.

PAINTING

NOW THAT YOU HAVE PREPARED YOUR ROOM FOR PAINTING, GATHERED THE BEST TOOLS FOR THE JOB, AND HAVE SELECTED THE RIGHT PAINT FOR YOUR PARTICULAR PROJECT, IT'S TIME TO START. Note that these instructions should be used whenever you apply a base coat to a wall for any of the techniques covered in this book. If you are painting a surface other than drywall, see page 22 for special preparation information.

When you begin keep in mind that working in a well-ventilated area will reduce adverse affects from paint fumes (even latex paints will have an odor in a small enclosed space). To keep a room well ventilated, open windows and turn on fans. Consider wearing a

paint **additives**

Before you paint, think about these products that can help with common problems:

paint extenders and conditioners: If
you have problems with brush marks showing while painting, try a paint extender, which conditions the paint and will improve brushability and workability.

mildew-preventing: If you are painting an
area that has a tendency to become wet, for instance a

bathroom, kitchen, basement, or laundry room, you may want to consider using a mildewcide.

Mildewcide is a chemical additive that prevents mildew from growing on paint, although it doesn't kill existing mildew. It usually comes in liquid form and can be added to paint—although extreme caution is recommended when adding and mixing. Paint that already contains mildewcide is more effective than adding it yourself; check paint labels to see if the paint you have chosen contains the additive.

paint finishes

PAINT—BOTH LATEX AND ALKYD—GENERALLY COMES IN FOUR FINISHES: FLAT, EGGSHELL, SEMI-GLOSS, AND GLOSS. Paint finishes are measured in degree of gloss, or sheen. The finish has nothing to do with the actual color of a paint, just how much light it reflects. When selecting a finish keep in mind that the higher the gloss is, the more durable it is. If you are painting over an already painted surface, you can paint gloss paint over a glossy surface, but you must first dull the surface with sandpaper so the top coat has something to hold onto.

flat paint has no glossy finish. As the least reflective of all finishes it is a duller finish and hides imperfections. Modern flat paint is easier to clean than in the past, but it won't withstand repeated washing and wear. Use flat paint on ceilings and walls in living rooms, bedrooms, and dining rooms. As a rule it offers easier, better coverage than other finishes and costs less.

eggshell finish, also known as satin and low-lustre, is between flat and semi-gloss. Use this sheen where you would use flat but want easier cleanup, such as in kids' rooms.

semi-gloss is more reflective than eggshell and should be used on kitchen and bathroom walls that will be exposed to moisture. Keep in mind that a semi-gloss or gloss sheen may appear a shade lighter than your paint chip because of the way it reflects light.

gloss is the most durable and stain-resistant sheen of all. This finish is best for high-traffic and dirty areas because it cleans the easiest, but it is also most likely to highlight surface imperfections. Use semi-gloss or gloss on trim, doors, and cabinets.

---

dust mask and goggles to prevent eye and lung irritation.

Stir the paint well with a paint stirrer or a mixing attachment for an electric drill. Make sure to stir from the bottom of the can to mix the clearer layer at the top with the heavier pigmented material that often settles at the bottom of the can.

If you are painting the ceiling of a room, paint it before the walls. Use a 2½- or 3-inch angled brush to outline the ceiling. This technique is known as "cutting in." Paint the ceiling with a roller and an extension handle to avoid standing on a ladder. If the ceiling is

TIPS for success

▪ If a paint drip has hardened on a wall, sand or scrape it down. If it's still tacky press a piece of masking tape gently over the flaw, then pull it off. Once the paint is dry, sand smooth and touch up with fresh paint.

◄ Holding a brush correctly is one of the keys to successful painting—and it reduces hand fatigue.

◄ For a clean edge use an angle-bristle brush when cutting in. Also leave an "airy" edge as shown that allows the trimmed portion to blend in when you paint the entire wall, rather than a crisp line that will be more visible—and more difficult to cover.

estimating paint for your job

▌ To determine how much paint you'll need for any project, measure all walls in the room. Add the lengths of the walls and multiply the total by the floor-to-ceiling height to get the square footage. To include the ceiling multiply the length of the room by its width. Add this number to the total square footage of the walls. Subtract 20 square feet for each door and 15 square feet for each window. Divide the result by the spreading rate of the paint (shown on the label; usually 400 square feet per gallon) to figure the gallons needed.

highly textured, you may need to use a paint sprayer, which is a powered tool that allows you to spray paint onto a surface with a hose and nozzle.

Like ceilings, you will need to cut in all walls. Cutting in is used for sharp edges around windows, where a wall meets the ceiling and other walls, and around moldings. Use an angle-bristle brush for this purpose to ensure a clean edge in areas that may be difficult to reach with a roller. To paint dampen the brush slightly with water; blot off any excess. Load the brush by dipping one-third of its bristles into the paint. Lift the bristles out of the paint, then gently tap them against the paint can's rim to remove excess paint (paint should not be dripping from

the bristles). Cut in around all walls and openings; let dry. Cut in again for a second coat if necessary; let dry.

After the second coat of trim paint has dried, it is time to fill in the outlined area with a roller. Dampen the roller slightly. Dip the roller in a tray full of paint and roll it up the tray's ramp until the cover is saturated, but not dripping. Paint strokes in a "W" pattern for even coverage and distribution of the paint. Once a wall is entirely covered with diagonal strokes, use long floor-to-ceiling strokes to fill in any uncovered areas. As you roll the paint on, be sure to overlap still-wet areas to prevent visible roll marks. After each wall is painted, let dry. Make sure the surfaces are dry before painting a second coat, or a topcoat as many of the techniques in this book require. A premature second coat could lift up the first coat.

As soon as you are finished painting, peel away the painter's tape from the molding and trim. This will allow you to clean up any smears on the molding while they are still wet.

Before cleaning up and storing your tools, take a step back and evaluate your work. If you see errant splotches on the ceiling, for example, or areas that didn't receive even coverage, touch them up now.

▲ Start painting strokes in a "W" pattern, then fill in any gaps with floor-to-ceiling strokes.

painting special surfaces

concrete: Thoroughly clean the concrete using a scrub brush. If there are any oily spots, apply a degreasing solution according to the product directions; let dry. Use either epoxy paints, which dry to a very hard finish and come in both water- and oil-base formulas, or cement paints. To prevent backaches from bending over when painting a concrete floor, use a roller with an extension handle.

laminate countertops: Painting these surfaces should be considered a temporary measure because of the high wear they receive. For longest wear use a special laminate paint, or use epoxy paint or a bonding primer beneath wall paint.

masonry: You can paint brick, stucco, and concrete block using the same procedure as for concrete. First use a stiff brush to remove dirt and chalk. You can also thoroughly clean the surface with a trisodium phosphate (TSP) cleaner and a wire brush. Avoid painting masonry less than 30 days old. If you must, wet it down with a hose and brush on acrylic sealer while the surface is still wet (remember this isn't necessary for new masonry older than 30 days). When the surface is dry, paint it with a high-quality latex floor paint.

tile: Choose epoxy paint for maximum adhesion to nonporous surfaces such as ceramic tile, or use a bonding primer beneath gloss or semi-gloss latex paint. Painted tile is more likely to endure on a wall than on a countertop or entryway floor. For even coverage paint the grout and the tiles rather than attempting to paint just the tiles.

vinyl floor: First prep the floor with a TSP cleaner; this will take the gloss off the vinyl surface and help the paint to adhere. Apply a stain-blocking primer and paint with an extremely durable acrylic paint. On vinyl flooring use wall paint or porch-and-deck paint topped with several coats of clear polyurethane. An additional top coat every couple of years will ensure its durability and cleanability.

wallpaper: If you can remove wallpaper and paste, do so. If not, wallpaper can usually be painted over with excellent results. First spot test the wallpaper in an inconspicuous area to make sure it won't loosen when covered with primer and paint. Repair bubbles by slicing them open and then gluing them down. Flake off peeling edges and feather with surfacing compound. Use a stain-blocking primer to ensure that the wallpaper color does not bleed through the paint; use either latex or alkyd paint.

wood floors, patios, and decks: Some manufacturers make latex or alkyd paints specially formulated for floor surfaces (the paint's binder is harder than in wall paint). Many floor paint lines come only in factory colors, so if you want a custom color, an alternative is to use wall paint topped with several layers of clear polyurethane. To paint outdoor projects, start with two coats of stain-blocking primer tinted to match your paint color, add your decorative painting, and seal and protect wood from outdoor elements with a coat of varnish.

wood paneling: Begin by removing any dirt or wax buildup with a high-strength household cleaner; rinse. Dull the glossy surface with sandpaper. Wipe with a damp rag to remove residue. Coat the surface with a stain-blocking primer; let dry. For the top coat use latex paint in a flat, satin, or semi-gloss finish.

wood veneer: If the veneer is solidly adhered, you can paint the surface. Begin by removing any dirt or wax buildup; rinse. Use fine sandpaper to dull the surface so the paint will adhere. Wipe with a damp rag to remove residue. Apply a stain-blocking primer tinted to match your paint color; let dry. Finish with latex paint in a flat, satin, or semi-gloss finish.

tools that make painting easier

specially designed roller covers with nap running around the end that allow you to paint in corners.

paint mixer attachment for a drill makes mixing quick and easy—and eliminates the need for wood and plastic stir sticks.

reusable paint can covers help reduce mess and waste when you pour paint from the can into a paint tray.

Look for **paints formulated to prepare damaged walls** for painting and for those that are mildew-fighting.

plastic paint tray liners are inexpensive and make cleanup a snap: These disposable liners can be thrown away after use, eliminating the need to scrub paint from a paint tray.

CLEANUP

AFTER YOU'VE FINISHED PAINTING BE SURE TO CLEAN AND STORE YOUR TOOLS PROPERLY. Remove as much paint as possible from brushes or rollers by drawing a brush comb or wire brush through the bristles. Then work the bristles back and forth across newspaper. Wash the brush under running water, bending the bristles back and forth in the palm of your hand to work out all traces of paint. Always let the water run from the handle down to the bristles. Hang brushes and roller covers to dry completely, combing the bristles so they are straight. When dry, wrap brushes and roller covers in their original plastic sleeves, kraft paper, or foil.

If you keep the paint used, tightly seal the can and store it upside down to prevent a top skin from forming. If you want to dispose of leftover latex paint, remove the lid from the can and air-dry it away from children and pets. To speed the drying process, add cat litter. Discard dry paint with normal trash. If you have empty cans, clean them and put them in a recycling bin. If you have leftover alkyd paint, take it to a toxic waste drop-off center or to a household materials recycling center where unused paints are recycled.

specialty paints

blackboard: Making a custom blackboard is quick and easy with spray or brush-on paints, available in both green and black.

cement: Tough, durable paints specially formulated for concrete give the look of natural stone, granite, limestone, and marble.

ceramic and porcelain: Hard-wearing, easy-to-clean paints for ceramic and porcelain surfaces in high-moisture areas offer a great way to revitalize worn surfaces.

epoxy: Epoxy paint can be used on numerous surfaces, including tiles and indoor metal appliances.

magnetic: Anyone can create a magnetic surface on walls and furnishings with magnetic paint. Available in spray and can formulas, this paint may be top-coated with another color of paint for a true custom look. It's perfect for kids' rooms and play spaces.

textured: These paints come in both spray and can forms. Textured spray paints are typically used for home decorating accessories and come in many colors and finishes. For walls, look for specialty paints that either contain additives to create a texture (for instance a granite look) or are formulated to be applied with specific tools to get a textural appearance (such as a suede finish).

TECHNIQUE PRIMER

THE FOLLOWING CHART WILL BE VERY USEFUL AS YOU BEGIN YOUR JOURNEY WITH COLOR AND DECORATIVE PAINTING TECHNIQUES.

This combines all of the information contained within each technique, but in a handy format that will help you to make color and paint selections for your particular ability level and the room or project you are painting.

	TECHNIQUE	DIFFICULTY	GLAZE	TOP COAT	BASE COAT	COLORS
32	COLORWASHING	Easy	Yes	Satin or Semi-Gloss	Satin or Semi-Gloss	Any; Light Base, Dark Top
38	FRESCO	Advanced	Yes	Satin or Semi-Gloss	Satin or Semi-Gloss	Similar Shades; Light Base, Dark Top
42	DENIM	Intermediate	Yes	Satin or Semi-Gloss	Satin or Semi-Gloss	White Base; Any Top
46	DRAGGING	Intermediate	Yes	Satin or Semi-Gloss	Satin or Semi-Gloss	Low- to Medium-Contrast
50	LINEN	Intermediate	Yes	Satin or Semi-Gloss	Satin or Semi-Gloss	Any; Light Base, Dark Top
56	LEATHER	Intermediate	Yes	Satin or Semi-Gloss	Satin or Semi-Gloss	Similar Shades; Light Base, Dark Top
60	FROTTAGE	Intermediate	Yes	Satin or Semi-Gloss	Satin or Semi-Gloss	Similar Shades or High-Contrast
64	RAGGING	Easy	Yes	Satin or Semi-Gloss	Satin or Semi-Gloss	Similar Shades or High-Contrast
70	SPONGING	Easy	Yes	Satin or Semi-Gloss	Satin or Semi-Gloss	Similar Shades or Tones
76	BURLAP, PINSTRIPES, MOIRÉ	Intermediate/Advanced	Yes	Satin or Semi-Gloss	Satin or Semi-Gloss	Any
86	STRIPES	Easy	Optional	Any Finish	Any Finish	Any
94	BLOCKS, GRIDS, CHECKS, GINGHAM	Intermediate	Optional	Any Finish	Any Finish	Any
106	DIAMONDS	Advanced	Optional	Any Finish	Any Finish	Any
112	PLAIDS	Advanced	Optional	Any Finish	Any Finish	Any
118	CALLIGRAPHY	Intermediate	No	Acrylic Paint or Paint Pen	Any Finish	Any
122	HAND-PAINTED MOTIFS	Intermediate	No	Acrylic Paint or Paint Pen	Any Finish	Any
128	STAMPING	Easy	Optional	Acrylic Paint	Any Finish	Any
134	STENCILING	Easy	Optional	Acrylic Paint or Cream	Any Finish	Any
146	MARBLING	Advanced	Optional	Latex and Acrylic Paints	Satin or Semi-Gloss	Earth Tones to Imitate Real Marble
150	WOOD GRAINING	Intermediate	Optional	Satin or Semi-Gloss	Satin or Semi-Gloss	Any; Low- to Medium-Contrast
154	DISTRESSING	Intermediate	No	Any Finish	Any Finish	Any; Medium- to High-Contrast
160	CRACKLING	Easy	No	Flat or Eggshell	Flat or Eggshell	Any; Medium- to High-Contrast
164	WHITEWASHING	Easy	No	Any Finish	n/a	White
168	DOUBLE-BRUSH, DOUBLE-ROLL	Intermediate	No	Any Finish	Any Finish	Any; Low- to Medium-Contrast
172	RECESSED DETAILS	Intermediate	Yes	Semi-Gloss	Semi-Gloss	Any; Low- to Medium-Contrast
178	DECOUPAGE	Easy	Optional	n/a	Any Finish	Any
184	TORN PAPER	Easy	No	n/a	n/a	Any

TOOLS	DECORATING STYLE	OTHER NOTES
Brush, Rag, or Sea Sponge	Any	Good background for other techniques or in geometric designs
Brush	Any	Colorwash is applied over joint compound; great for damaged walls
Weaver Brush, Check Roller	Casual, Informal	Distinct woven texture; produce in panels with "seams"
Strié Brush	Any	Small spaces are more manageable
Weaver Brush	Any	Distinct woven texture
Plastic Bags, Sheets, or Wrap	Casual, "Rugged" Look	Great for walls and wood furnishings with flat panels
Newsprint, Kraft Paper, or Newspaper	Casual, Contemporary	Highly textured pattern
Rag or Ragging Mitt	Any	Can appear busy in small spaces; choose colors with care
Sea Sponge or Sponging Mitt	Casual	Great impact when used sparingly
Comb or Squeegee	Any	Need steady hand; can make comb for custom motif widths
Colored Pencils, Measuring Tools, Tape	Any	Can combine with other techniques; tape for crisp lines or hand-paint
Colored Pencils, Measuring Tools, Tape	Any	Great for focal-point wall; can combine with other techniques
Colored Pencils, Measuring Tools, Tape	Any	Great for focal-point wall; can combine with other techniques
Colored Pencils, Measuring Tools, Tape	Casual	Great for focal-point wall and wood furnishings with flat panels
Carbon Copy Paper, Pencil	Any	Can hand-letter, stencil, or use projector instead of carbon copy paper
Paint Pens or Markers	Casual	Practice motifs on a sample board before painting project
Foam Stamps	Any	Can make custom stamps; stamp in random or border pattern
Stencils, Stenciling Brushes	Any	Can make custom stencils; stencil in random or border pattern
Plastic Wrap, Softening Brush, Feather	Formal/Traditional	Small spaces are more manageable; incorporates leather technique
Wood-Graining Tool	Any	Small spaces are more manageable
Sandpaper, Stain	Casual, Cottage	Aged, antiqued look; great for walls and wood furnishings
Crackle Medium, Brush or Sea Sponge	Casual, Cottage	Top splits and cracks to reveal base; great for walls and wood furnishings
Brush, Rag	Casual, Cottage	Use on unfinished wood surface, including beaded board and floors
Double-Brush or Double-Roller, Tray	Casual	Pleasing blended finish; choose colors with care
Embossed Wallpaper, Squeegee	Any	Great visual depth; raised details stand out against dark recessed areas
Decoupage Papers, Decoupage Medium	Any	Can cover decoupaged surface with glaze/paint mixture
Prepasted Patterned Wallpaper	Any	When wallpaper is torn and adhered to wall, it resembles faux finish

Create TE

TURE with

Glazes

GLAZE—*paint without pigment*—is the true workhorse of the decorative painting world: When mixed with any paint color, **it alters** the paint's consistency and drying time, enabling you to **create an infinite array of textures** on walls and other paintable surfaces. The amount of glaze and the tools used will affect your results. In this section **you will learn how to use this versatile medium** to master a wide range of techniques from familiar sponging and popular ragging to unconventional frottage and highly textured burlap.

Introduction to GLAZES

GLAZE IS ONE OF THE MOST ESSENTIAL MEDIUMS USED IN DECORATIVE PAINTING: It allows paint to stay wet and workable longer than if the paint were used alone and adds depth and dimension to paintable surfaces. The amount and type of glaze (tinted or untinted), as well as the tools used to apply or remove it, will affect the final look. When one layer of glaze is applied over a solid color, it results in a sheen, highlighting the base coat color (as in the red portion of the bedroom wall, opposite ▶). When tinted glazes are layered atop one another, the colors merge for a rich effect (as on the coffee table top, below ➡).

When you choose glazes to use for a particular project, it is important to understand the types of glazes available and how they work. While traditional alkyd (oil-base) glazes have been the chosen medium for decorative painting, they can be hazardous to use. Alkyd glazes stay wet and workable for long periods of time and result in a durable finish, but both the chemicals used in the glaze and the fumes can pose a health threat. In recent years good-quality acrylic or latex (water-base) glazes have been introduced, which are safer for you and the environment. Cleanup is a snap with water and, if durability is a concern, a clear sealer can be applied over

This sturdy coffee table top has the appearance of burled wood. Accomplish this look by applying reddish-brown and medium brown glazes in a crosshatched, or "X," pattern over a light beige base coat. While the glazes are wet, roll a piece of cheesecloth into a ball and dab onto the surface to soften the look and remove obvious brushstrokes. Apply a coat of polyurethane to help the table withstand everyday use.

A soft, mottled effect—achieved by sponging diluted white glaze over painted and stamped walls—adds depth and dimension to this bedroom. The rich treatment is the ideal backdrop for the homemade, not-quite-perfect flower and paisley stamped designs. See page 128 for more information on stamping.

the painted surface. All of the techniques featured in this section use water-base glazes; if you choose to use oil-base products, make sure to read and follow all package directions carefully.

One of the keys to working successfully with glazes is understanding the glaze/paint ratio. The more glaze you add to the paint, the more transparent, or clear, it will be. And the more transparent the mixture, the more the base coat (or previous layers of glazes) will show through. Conversely, when less glaze is added, the more opaque (nontransparent) it will be—and the more it will cover the base coat color.

Introduction to GLAZES *continued*

There is no magic recipe for mixing glaze and paint: You will require different levels of transparency or opaqueness for various techniques and effects. As a starting point mix 4 parts glaze to 1 part paint in a bucket or paint tray; if desired add 1 part water for increased translucency and/or 1 ounce of gel retarder per gallon of paint to extend the drying time. Before undertaking a project, try out your mixture on a primed sample board; adjust the mixture as needed for the desired effect. Once you find the perfect ratio, make sure to write it down for future reference.

the wisdom of **sample boards**

■ When you are ready to undertake any of the decorative painting techniques featured in this book, especially those that require the use of glazes, first practice the technique on a foam core sample board that has been base-coated like your wall or project surface. This will give you the opportunity to become familiar with the technique and specialty tools, and even to experiment with glaze/paint ratios before making a commitment to your walls or other surfaces.

GLAZE BASICS

■ Apply a base coat of interior satin or semi-gloss paint beneath a glaze/paint top coat; these paints have a sheen that helps to show off the decorative paint treatment. Don't use flat paint, because glazes do not slide easily over it and flat paint will soak up the glaze.

■ For consistent results don't overload application tools, including brushes, rollers, rags, and sponges, with glaze.

■ While glaze extends the drying time of paint, you still need to work quickly; glaze becomes unworkable in about 15 minutes unless a paint conditioner, such as gel retarder, is added. For best results work within 3- to 4-foot square or vertical areas, leaving a "soft" edge that will be easy to blend. Working with a partner may also contribute to more consistent results.

■ You can mix any paint color with glaze to create a custom look. While premixed color glazes are available, they are expensive and the color palette is limited.

■ Cover the glaze/paint mixture with a lid or plastic wrap while painting to prevent the glaze from drying out.

■ When layering glazes, select colors that complement each other and will combine to make an interesting, pleasing effect.

The beauty of aged finishes—or those that appear aged—is in the paint layers that wear away in spots to reveal subtle colors. In this dining area a top coat of green glaze is applied unevenly over a yellow base coat, allowing the base coat to "peek out"; then some of the glaze is removed with a combination of combing and "negative" stenciling (rather than applying paint in the stencil's openings, it is removed). See page 76 for more information on combing and page 134 for more information on stenciling.

COLORWASHING

ONE OF THE MOST VERSATILE of all decorative painting techniques, colorwashing offers a wide range of looks and styles, from subtle, soft, and watery to dramatic and aged. For this technique you apply thin layers of color with a brush, rag, sponge, or even unconventional tools like a feather duster. Colorwashing can stand on its own in nearly any setting, from country to traditional, and it is a wonderful textured background for many of the techniques featured in Section Three, including hand-painted motifs, stamping, and stenciling.

Colorwashing can be done with watered-down paint, or even undiluted paint, but adding glaze to the paint will result in a richer quality—and makes the process much easier because of the longer drying time. The recommended ratio is 4 parts glaze to 1 part paint, but experiment to find the right amount of translucency or opaqueness for your particular project. For increased translucency, add water to the mixture.

colorwashed stripes

▲ Two different blue glazes are applied over a white base coat in alternating 8-inch stripes. The stripes are crisp but don't appear too formal.

Colorwashing can stand on its own in nearly any setting and is a wonderful textured background for other techniques.

▲ Colorwashed stripes add textural interest to this bedroom but don't overpower it: The subtle blues almost fade away to emphasize the bed, mosaic mirror, and lively artwork. This bedroom is youthful and fun, but stripes, especially those that are richly colorwashed, work equally as well in cottage or contemporary settings. See page 86 for more information on stripes.

colorwashing the blues

SOFT BLUES INTERMINGLE on the walls of this dining area. The delicate effect is perfect for casual, informal spaces. Above the chair rail molding, a light blue colorwash is applied over an off-white base coat. Below, the same blue pairs with a darker blue glaze/paint mixture for a playful checkerboard effect. See page 94 for more information on check designs.

contrasting **colorwashes**

▼ The chair rail molding in this living room provides the perfect divider to change color intensity. The same light green paint covers the entire wall, but above the chair rail a mixture of 4 parts glaze to 1 part paint is applied. Below the chair rail the mixture is 1 part glaze to 1 part paint. A brush is used in a crosshatching motion to colorwash the mixtures above and below the chair rail.

quick and easy **colorwash**

▲ This bathroom was painted in less than an hour using a colorwashing kit. The range of yellows brings warmth and depth to this small space.

COLORWASH FROM a **BOX**

■ If you love the look of colorwashed walls, but you are uneasy about getting the glaze/paint mixture just right, don't sweat it: There are new products available that eliminate the guesswork, making the process fun and simple. The kit used in the bathroom *above* comes with a water-base paint, a cotton application cloth, and latex-free gloves. The paint is simply mixed with water in the desired ratio (the more water added, the lighter the mixture) and wiped on with the cloth in figure-eight and circular motions over a white base coat.

the COLORWASHING technique

■ You can apply a colorwash over nearly any base coat color, but light colors like white or off-white tend to work best. The glaze/paint mixture will have more depth—from light to dark—when applied over a light color. If you prefer, use a dark base coat and apply glaze alone as a top coat.

You can use a wide variety of tools for the colorwashing technique. A brush will create uneven streaks, while a sea sponge will produce a softer look when applied in circular strokes. Applying the glaze/paint mixture with varying pressures will affect the final appearance. Experiment with different tools, pressures, and glaze/paint ratios on a primed sample board to determine the best effect for your particular project.

YOU WILL NEED

- ☐ **Satin or semi-gloss latex paint for base coat in desired color**
- ☐ **Satin or semi-gloss latex paint for top coat in desired color**
- ☐ **Glaze**
- ☐ **Paintbrush or roller and paint tray**
- ☐ **Bucket and mixing tool**
- ☐ **Application tool, such as a sea sponge, rag, or brush**

HOW-TO steps

1. Apply the base coat to the surface; let dry.

2. Mix the glaze and top coat paint in the desired ratio. Water may be added for increased translucency.

3. If using a sea sponge or rag, apply the glaze/paint mixture to an approximate 4-foot square section of the wall, rubbing it over the area in a circular or figure-eight motion. If using a brush or other similar tool, apply the mixture to the wall in a crosshatching "X" motion. (**Photo A**) Note that when using a brush in a crosshatching motion, all brushstrokes will be seen if you are painting on a smooth wall; the more textured the wall, the less noticeable the brushstrokes will be.

4. After the 4-foot square section is complete, immediately begin applying the glaze/paint mixture in an adjacent 4-foot square section. Blend and smooth the areas between the sections while the glaze from the previous section is still wet and workable. Continue the process until the entire wall is complete.

Ⓐ

TIPS for success

■ Colorwashing is an ideal technique to use on walls that are not in perfect condition: Its textured appearance will help hide blemishes, turning rough, inconsistent walls into a surface rich with color.

FRESCO

FRESCO, THAT CLASSIC PAINT TECHNIQUE made famous by Greeks and Romans centuries ago, was traditionally created by painting a mixture of water and pigments over wet lime plaster. Fresco is usually thought of—and seen—in rooms with old world charm and in a terra-cotta color. Today an equally handsome, aged appearance can be created by simply applying a colorwash over a thin layer of drywall joint compound or plaster. The drywall compound will fill any imperfections, like nail holes, on your walls—and even camouflage large cracks and heavily damaged walls—and the uneven texture enhances the fresco technique: Rich color will settle into the crevices, giving a greater appearance of depth than if colorwashing alone were applied. The resulting layers of color and texture complement artwork, collections, and furnishings of nearly any style. See page 32 for information on colorwashing.

▲ The fresco technique can be successfully used in any room of the home with any style of decoration. The faded blues in this living room provide a subtle backdrop for the clean-line, contemporary furnishings and accessories. The wall texture adds warmth and interesting pattern to the space.

project: tinted plaster

While many decorative painting techniques hint at texture, layering pigmented plaster on a wall truly gives it dimension. This technique is almost true to the original method of painting on a layer of moist lime plaster; instead you will be mixing the paint and plaster and applying it to a wall. You will need two colors of paint to mix with the plaster: Select colors within the same family (for instance yellow and orange) for the most pleasing finished look. Keep in mind that while the results are spectacular, this process is more time-intensive than paint-only techniques.

HOW-TO steps

1. Mix plaster and latex paint, adding small amounts of paint until the desired base coat color is achieved. Note that the color will lighten as the plaster dries.

2. Using a trowel apply a thin coat of the mixture to the wall in small sections, overlapping and leaving slight bumps and ripples to add depth to the finish. Let the plaster mixture dry at least 24 hours.

3. Mix plaster with another color of paint and apply in the same way, leaving some of the base coat layer to be exposed, if desired. Repeat the process with as many colors and layers as needed to achieve the desired look.

4. When the plaster is dry, sand the walls with fine sandpaper, rubbing off patches of the top coat of plaster to smooth out the peaks and give the finish an aged look.

▲ The walls of this breakfast room have a time-weathered look, achieved with layers of plaster pigmented with ocher and terra cotta. The overall rustic European farmhouse flavor is achieved with the "aged" walls, peasant-style tablecloth, and pine furnishings.

▲ Patchy, uneven layers of butterscotch, terra-cotta, and teal-color plaster give the walls of this sophisticated dining room the look of a shabby-chic Mediterranean villa.

basic wall texturing

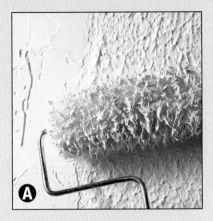

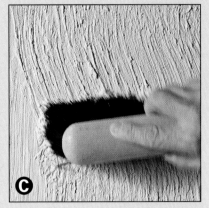

BRAND-NEW WALLS CAN ACQUIRE INSTANT CHARACTER with an easy-to-apply wall texture. You can use any of the following methods for applying drywall joint compound or plaster for the fresco technique. Don't limit yourself. The depth achieved by textured walls can enhance any painted surface.

SPACKLING KNIFE: This is the most basic application method. Use the knife to apply the compound to the wall. Smooth the surface lightly, then press the knife to the wall and lift it away to create a stucco surface. You can either leave the surface as is or use one of the following methods to create other designs. You may also use a plaster trowel to apply the compound.

BRUSH ROLLER: After applying the compound, and while it is still wet, use a high-nap roller to create a dappled effect. (Photo A)

KNIFE: To capture the look and feel of old plaster, run a roller over the compound while it is still wet, then lightly go over it with a flat side of a broad knife.

SANDPAPER: After rolling over the compound, allow it to dry, then lightly sand the high tips and rough spots for a smoother look. (Photo B)

BRUSH: Rather than using a roller to create the texture, try using a stiff, dry brush over the wet compound to create rhythmic designs of your choice, including swirls, waves, and stripes. (Photo C)

the **FRESCO** technique

■ You will need to choose two colors for this technique, both of which will be applied over a thin layer of drywall joint compound. Select colors that complement each other and will blend to produce a pleasing result, for instance light and medium shades of yellow, orange, or blue. As in colorwashing, choose a light color for the base coat that will allow the glaze/paint mixture to best show its depth.

One of the keys to executing the fresco technique successfully is keeping the joint compound layer thin: If it is too thick, it will crack. The compound has a tendency to dry quickly, so you will need to work with some speed to get the desired texture.

YOU WILL NEED

☐ **Drywall joint compound**

☐ **Plaster trowel or spackling knife**

☐ **Sandpaper**

☐ **Dust mask**

☐ **Drywall primer**

☐ **³/₄-inch high-nap roller and paint tray**

☐ **Satin or semi-gloss latex paint for base coat in desired color**

☐ **Satin or semi-gloss latex paint for top coat in desired color**

☐ **Glaze**

☐ **Bucket and mixing tool**

☐ **Paintbrushes**

HOW-TO steps

1. Apply a thin ¹/₈- to ³/₈-inch layer of drywall joint compound to the wall, starting at an upper corner. To obtain a rough surface, use random, sweeping motions as you apply the compound.

2. Allow the drywall compound to dry completely. While wearing a dust mask, sand down any protruding ridges or peaks. Vacuum and dust any resulting particles.

3. Apply a primer suitable for drywall to the walls with a high-nap (³/₄-inch) roller; let dry.

4. Apply the base coat to the surface; let dry.

5. Mix 4 parts glaze to 1 part top coat paint.

6. With random brushstrokes, apply the glaze/paint mixture to an approximate 2-foot square section, leaving some of the base coat exposed, if desired. (Photo A)

7. Continue working down or across the wall in approximate 2-foot square sections, applying the glaze/paint mixture and blending as you go. Be sure to blend the edges of adjoining sections; working with a partner will help ensure smooth transitions between the areas.

Ⓐ

DENIM

THE LOOK OF DENIM, THAT ALL-AMERICAN FABRIC, can give your walls a lived-in, casual appearance that is perfect for informal living areas like bedrooms, baths, and even dining rooms. Whether executed in light blue, deep indigo, or even unconventional red or green, the technique produces a woven texture that livens up a room, especially one that lacks architectural details. Don't limit yourself to walls only: The technique can give a handsome time-worn look to furniture too.

The technique is similar in nature to other "woven fabric" techniques, including dragging, featured on page 46, and linen, beginning on page 50, where a top coat glaze/paint mixture is applied over a base coat and partially removed with a wide, stiff-bristle weaver brush. To further emphasize the rough, woven effect, a check roller (see page 45 for more information) is used after the surface has been brushed.

TIPS for success

▌ For added detail and a more authentic look, hand-paint faux "stitch marks" over the seam lines of the denim panels.

▲ Detail of a "seam" and heavily textured crosshatched pattern in the bathroom *opposite.*

bathed in **denim**

▲ Rich cobalt blue livens up the walls of this otherwise ordinary bathroom. The crosshatched pattern breaks up the color and creates the subtle denimlike panels. The "seams" are achieved by completing the treatment in long vertical sections and overlapping the edges slightly. To add even more interest to the room, the ceiling is given a ragging-on treatment: A dark green glaze/paint mixture is applied with a rag over a light green base coat. For information on ragging, see page 64.

denim makes a bold statement in red

▲ Who says denim has to be blue? A vibrant red is used on this dining room wall. It provides the perfect backdrop for clean, simple line white dishes and a plate rack. The woven denim pattern is achieved by working wet glaze with a weaver brush and check roller.

the DENIM technique

■ While the denim technique may look daunting, working in sections makes it quite manageable. As with most techniques that incorporate glazes, you will need to work quickly in each section: You need to brush the glaze in both a horizontal and vertical direction, then use a check roller—all while the glaze is wet. Depending on the size of the sections with which you choose to work, working with a partner may help speed the process, which is helpful when working with quick-drying glazes.

YOU WILL NEED

- ☐ **Satin or semi-gloss latex paint for base coat, white**
- ☐ **Satin or semi-gloss latex paint for top coat in desired color**
- ☐ **Glaze**
- ☐ **Painter's tape**
- ☐ **Roller and paint tray**
- ☐ **Bucket and mixing tool**
- ☐ **Weaver brush**
- ☐ **Check roller**
- ☐ **Lint-free cloth**

HOW-TO steps

1. Paint the walls with the white latex paint; let dry.

2. Divide the room into a series of vertical sections, narrow enough that you can work the section from top to bottom quickly, but not so narrow that you create more "seams," or vertical lines, than are visually pleasing. Mask off alternating sections using painter's tape.

3. Mix 1 part glaze to 3 parts top coat paint.

4. Roll the glaze/paint mixture onto one section of the wall. While the glaze is still wet, stroke the weaver brush down the length of the entire section (vertically) and then horizontally. (Photo A) Wipe the brush with a lint-free cloth after each stroke to remove excess glaze.

5. Using the check roller apply firm pressure and roll the tool over the brushed section, vertically and then horizontally while the glaze is still wet and workable. (Photo B)

6. Repeat the process for every masked-off (alternating) section. Remove the tape; let the paint dry.

7. Mask off each unpainted section, positioning the tape about $^3/_8$ inch inside the edges of the previously painted sections. Paint the sections with the glaze/paint mixture in the same manner as described in Steps 4 and 5, painting over the $^3/_8$-inch sections to create "seams." Remove the tape; let the paint dry.

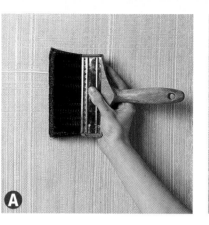

A

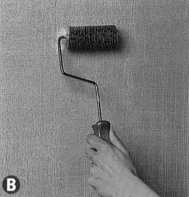

B

CHECK**ROLLER**

■ While you can achieve a **woven look** with a weaver brush alone, the use of a **check roller** will enhance the effect. Look for check rollers in home improvement centers and specialty paint stores.

DRAGGING (Strié)

DRAGGING, OR STRIÉ, IS THE PERFECT COMPLEMENT TO ANY SETTING where you desire a highly textured look: The resulting finish is similar to top-quality, traditional fabrics and wallcoverings. While it looks wonderful in formal settings, especially in deep reds, greens, and blues, it can be equally as attractive in neutrals for contemporary settings.

The dragging technique requires a steady hand—you drag a brush down or across a surface in one continuous stroke. Because of this, tackling a large or tall expanse of wall may prove difficult. Dragging is very effective in small spaces, which may prove more manageable, for instance, above or below a chair rail, within sections of molding on a wall, or on furniture or doors.

When choosing colors for the dragging technique, think

▲ The red strié treatment in this bedroom provides a rich, textural backdrop for artwork and traditional furnishings.

dragging in small spaces

▲ Dining rooms, living rooms, and bedrooms aren't the only spaces that will benefit from lavish paint treatments: Smaller informal areas, such as the bathroom *above* and *below*, can look equally as stunning when treated to a textural treatment like dragging.

LOW CONTRAST

MEDIUM CONTRAST

HIGH CONTRAST

▲ Different shades of green can combine for various effects.

about what you want the final effect to be, keeping in mind that the base coat color will be exposed as the top coat glaze/paint mixture is removed. If you want a subtle effect, select similar colors, or even different shades of one color (for example medium and dark yellow); if you desire more drama, choose high-contrast colors (like red and white).

When planning your project also keep in mind that you can get different effects based on the type of brush you use (see page 49 for options) and the number of times you pass over the same glazed section. The more you brush over the glaze, the lighter the effect will be, because you are

continuing to take off glaze and expose the base coat.

Regardless of what look you want, make sure you work on a smooth surface for an even, regular pattern.

dragging in neutral shades

THE CONTEMPORARY—YET CASUAL—
APPEARANCE of this entryway is achieved through
the use of neutral colors: cream and beige. While the
dragging technique results in a high texture, neutral
colors such as these result in a softer visual effect
that is perfect for relaxed settings.

the **DRAGGING** (Strié) technique

■ As with most "negative" techniques (where a glaze/top-coat paint mixture is removed from a surface), dragging can get quite messy, so be sure to protect your work area with drop cloths. To prevent your brush from becoming too overloaded—which can result in an uneven effect and even more mess—wipe away any excess glaze with a lint-free rag after each pass of the brush.

YOU WILL NEED

- ☐ Satin or semi-gloss latex paint for base coat in desired color
- ☐ Satin or semi-gloss latex paint for top coat in desired color
- ☐ Glaze
- ☐ Painter's tape
- ☐ Roller and paint tray
- ☐ Bucket and mixing tool
- ☐ Strié brush
- ☐ Lint-free cloth

HOW-TO steps

1. Apply the base coat to the surface; let dry.

2. Divide the room into a series of approximate 2- to 3-foot wide vertical sections. Mask off alternating sections using painter's tape.

3. Mix 4 parts glaze to 1 part top coat paint.

4. Roll the glaze/paint mixture onto one section of the wall. Starting at the top of the just-glazed section and using the strié brush, drag through the glaze vertically in one continuous stroke. Hold the brush at a comfortable angle and press the bristles firmly against the wall. **(Photo A)** Wipe the brush with a lint-free cloth after each stroke to remove excess glaze. Use the edge of the previous brush pass as a guide as you continue down the wall.

5. Repeat the process for every masked-off

Ⓐ

(alternating) section. Remove the tape; let the paint dry.

6. Mask off each unpainted section. Paint the sections with the glaze/paint mixture in the same manner as described in Step 4. Remove the tape; let the paint dry.

for success

■ A steady hand is important for techniques like dragging, especially if you plan to treat a large expanse of wall. If you have difficulty dragging the brush down the wall in one continuous motion, go as far as you can, and then drag from the bottom up to that point. To soften the meeting point, feather your brush as the lines meet. Staggering the meeting points will prevent the appearance of a horizontal line across the wall.

dragging brush options

■ There are myriad brushes and other tools that will work for the dragging technique. For best results use a wide strié brush with stiff bristles. Strié brushes **(A)** can be expensive, so experiment with less expensive options such as wallpaper brushes **(B)** or even nontraditional tools like coarse sponges **(C)**.

LINEN

REAL LINEN IS KNOWN FOR ITS STRENGTH, COOLNESS, AND COARSE WEAVE. You can duplicate the look of this crisp fabric with a wide, weaver brush and sweeping horizontal and vertical strokes. The technique is appropriate for any room in the home: It adds distinctive texture but doesn't compete with artwork and furnishings. While the linen treatment may look daunting, it is actually quite forgiving: Mistakes are easily dry-brushed out.

▲ Because the ceilings are high (11 feet) in this living room space, white moldings are added level with the window tops to even out the proportion and bring the eye down. Below the molding a light gray paint provides a neutral background for this country-inspired room, while above a beige linen pattern adds visual interest and draws the eye toward the playful checkerboard design on the ceiling. See page 94 for more information on creating a checkerboard pattern.

linen and adjoining rooms

▲ The blue linen treatment in this breakfast room gives the walls a slightly worn look, while bringing gentle color and pattern into the room. The coarse weave complements the room's architecture.

▲ The adjoining living room features the same blue linen look, but it is paired with pale yellow in alternating vertical stripes to make a smooth transition between the two spaces. See page 86 for more information on creating stripes.

For a light, open feel in cottage or country settings, choose neutral colors such as pale yellow and blue or traditional beige. For more drama in contemporary areas, try vivid shades of reds and pinks.

linen technique brush motion

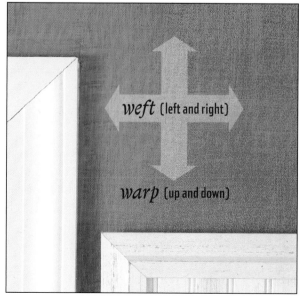

weft (left and right)

warp (up and down)

▲ The coarse warp (vertical) and weft (horizontal) pattern gives the linen technique its distinct look.

project: **linen** and stripes

Wide alternating stripes of the linen technique and deep parsley green call attention to the walls of this breezy bedroom. The stenciled ginko leaves add movement. The stencil shown is intended as an overall wall stencil, but it is used for random leaves—sparse at the top and middle, then more concentrated toward the bottom, as if they are falling into a pile. Leaves going off the edges add to the random look. For more information on creating stripes, see page 86; for further information on stenciling, see page 134.

YOU WILL NEED

- ☐ **Satin or semi-gloss latex paint for base coat in desired color**
- ☐ **Satin or semi-gloss latex paint for top coat in desired color**
- ☐ **Glaze**
- ☐ **Roller and paint tray**
- ☐ **6-inch weaver brush**
- ☐ **Painter's tape**
- ☐ **Lint-free rags**
- ☐ **Tape measure**
- ☐ **Carpenter's level**
- ☐ **Colored pencil (that matches paint)**
- ☐ **Ginko leaf stencil**
- ☐ **Stencil adhesive**
- ☐ **Paper plate**
- ☐ **Stenciling brush**
- ☐ **Paper towels**

HOW-TO steps

1. Apply the base coat to the surface; let dry.

2. Measure the width of each wall and divide by the number of stripes desired to determine the width of each stripe; mark the wall with the white colored pencil. **Note: The stripes shown are 24 inches wide.** Extend the lines with the colored pencil and carpenter's level.

3. Tape off each stripe with painter's tape.

4. Follow the instructions on page 55 for creating the linen look on alternating stripes; let dry.

5. Spray the back of the stencil with stencil adhesive and press onto the wall, within one of the linen sections. Put a little of the top coat paint onto the paper plate. Dip the stenciling brush into the paint, blotting any excess paint onto a paper towel. Using a pouncing motion, apply paint to the stencil openings. Reposition the stencil and continue stenciling leaves in the desired fashion.

6. Repeat Step 5 on all of the linen sections; let dry.

sophisticated linen

WHO SAYS LINEN HAS TO BE SUBTLE? This bright fuchsia treatment provides a dramatic, sophisticated backdrop for the crisp white cabinets, silver serving pieces and utensils, and botanical prints in this small multipurpose room, left and below. *The oversize checked window scarf and stenciled border keep the space from looking too serious. See page 134 for more information on stenciling.*

linen and lavender

TWO SHADES OF LAVENDER are used to produce the soft, pretty walls in this bedroom. A darker shade of paint is applied as the base coat, and a lighter shade is used as the top coat. The subtle texture of linen in two shades of one color creates a relaxed, harmonious feel. See page 102 for instructions on creating the gingham drawer fronts and page 92 for making a striped floorcloth.

the **LINEN** technique

■ Achieve the linen look with one of two methods: You can apply untinted glaze over any color of base coat paint for a translucent effect, or apply a glaze/dark paint mixture over a light base coat for more contrast.

Although glaze extends the drying time of paint, you need to work quickly for satisfactory results. While you can certainly work alone, for ease of completing either method, two people are preferred: One can apply the glaze and one can use the brush to create the linen look.

YOU WILL NEED

- ☐ Satin or semi-gloss latex paint for base coat in desired color
- ☐ Optional: Satin or semi-gloss latex paint for top coat in desired color
- ☐ Glaze
- ☐ 6-inch weaver brush
- ☐ Roller and paint tray
- ☐ Painter's tape
- ☐ Lint-free rags
- ☐ Tape measure

HOW-TO steps

1. Apply the base coat to the surface; let dry. (**Photo A**)

2. Divide the room into a series of vertical sections, narrow enough that you can work the section from top to bottom quickly, but not so narrow that you create more "seams," or vertical lines, than are visually pleasing. Using painter's tape, mask off every other section.

3. If using a different top coat paint color, mix 5 parts glaze to 1 part top coat paint.

4. Roll the glaze/paint mixture or glaze alone onto one section of the wall. While the glaze is still wet, use the weaver brush to make a horizontal stripe across the top of the section. (**Photo B**) Immediately brush in the opposite horizontal direction. Repeat, working quickly down the entire glazed section. Wipe the brush with a lint-free cloth after each stroke to remove excess glaze. (**Photo C**)

5. Make a vertical stroke, holding the brush straight. Repeat, working quickly across the entire section. (**Photo D**)

6. Repeat the process for every masked off (alternating) section. Remove the tape; let each section dry.

7. Mask off each unpainted section, positioning the tape about ³/₈ inch inside the edges of the previously painted sections. Paint the sections with the glaze/paint mixture in the same manner as described in Steps 4 and 5, painting over the ³/₈-inch sections to create "seams." Remove the tape; let the paint dry.

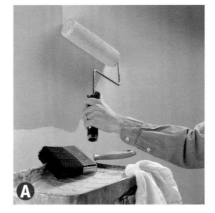
A

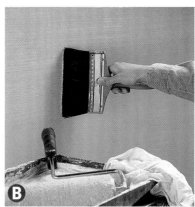
B

C

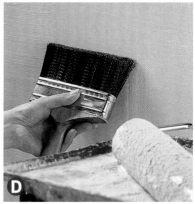
D

TIPS for success

■ To reduce possible smudging

drag out from corners,

rather than into them.

LEATHER

REAL LEATHER EXUDES THE RUGGED NATURE OF THE OUTDOORS. Creating the look of this handsome, masculine material on walls and other paintable surfaces is surprisingly easy with the help of common household plastic wrap or bags: After a top coat glaze/paint mixture is applied over a dried base coat, the plastic is smoothed on and peeled away to reveal the texture. The leather technique looks great in rustic cabinlike settings, where leather furniture and outdoor motifs are present, as well as in cozy home offices and dens.

▲ Besides walls, the highly textured leather technique works well on any flat, smooth surface, including furniture with simple, clean lines. Upholstery tacks add a masculine flair to the coffee table in this living room.

▲ A rugged leather technique is the perfect match for this living room, with its impressive stone fireplace and comfy leather furniture (shown in the photo *left*), keeping all elements "natural," from the wood and stone to the leather, woven baskets, and sisal rug. The technique is created in small, more manageable "panels"; the "seams" between the panels are highly visible in this living room.

LEATHER DOESN'T HAVE TO BE USED STRICTLY ON WALLS to be effective. Right *and* below, *a plain headboard and footboard are treated to the technique: A rich red base coat with a dark glaze/paint mixture creates this look. The raised edges of the pieces are distressed for even more rugged good looks. See page 154 for more information on distressing.*

head to toe in leather

To emulate real leather paint "marks" and "scars" on the base coat prior to applying the top coat glaze/paint mixture with a thin artist brush and a paint color darker than the base coat.

the soft look of **suede**

LIKE LEATHER, SUEDE HAS A
DISTINCT TEXTURE, albeit more
supple, that looks great in spaces
that feature handsome furnishings
and accessories. The textured walls
in this home office are created with a
specially formulated paint product
available at home improvement
centers. Crafts stores often carry
products that produce the look of
suede—and leather—right from the
can on everything from walls to
home decorating accessories.

◀ ▲ The mottled suede walls in this office are a soft, subtle backdrop for the leather-top desk.

the **LEATHER** technique

■ There are numerous ways to achieve the leather look—including the use of a stipple brush or chamois cloth to blend and remove some of the top coat glaze/paint mixture applied over a solid base coat—but the method described below is easier to master and will give more consistent results. Here, plastic—smoothed over the wet glaze/paint mixture and then peeled off—is used to obtain the texture. One caveat: The used plastic can cause quite a mess, so be sure to protect the floor and other surfaces with drop cloths.

Choose two colors for this technique; two shades of a color often work best. While it is most common to use a light base coat and darker top coat, experiment with different combinations on a primed sample board to find the most pleasing effect.

YOU WILL NEED

- ☐ Satin or semi-gloss latex paint for base coat in desired color
- ☐ Satin or semi-gloss latex paint for top coat in desired color
- ☐ Glaze
- ☐ Roller or paintbrush and paint tray
- ☐ Bucket and mixing tool
- ☐ Plastic drop cloths, bags, sheets, or wrap
- ☐ Tape measure
- ☐ Colored pencil, in color that matches base coat color
- ☐ Paper and pencil

HOW-TO steps

1. Apply the base coat to the surface; let dry.

2. Measure the height and width of each wall. Make a small sketch of each wall to these dimensions, dividing each wall into sections for the leather treatment that are visually pleasing. Measure and mark each wall where appropriate with the colored pencil. Using painter's tape, mask off every other section.

3. Cut a piece of plastic material 6 to 12 inches larger on each side than each section measured in Step 2.

4. Mix 4 parts glaze to 1 part top coat paint. Roll or brush onto one section of the wall.

5. While the top coat mixture is wet, press the appropriately sized piece of plastic onto the wall, smoothing it with your hand or a brush.

6. Carefully peel the plastic off the wall. (Photo A)

7. Continue working down or across the wall, applying the glaze/paint mixture to every masked off (alternating) section. Remember to use fresh plastic for each section. Remove the tape; let the paint dry.

8. Mask off each unpainted section. Paint the sections with the glaze/paint mixture in the same manner as described in Steps 5 through 7. Remove the tape; let the paint dry.

FROTTAGE

USING THE SAME BASIC PRINCIPLES AS THE LEATHER TECHNIQUE explained on page 59, frottage entails the use of newspaper, kraft paper, or unprinted newsprint rubbed over a wet glaze/paint top coat mixture.

Once the paper is pulled off, the surface is left with a random, patchy, highly textured pattern that looks especially at home in contemporary and casual settings.

▲ Casual elegance best describes the overall look of this living room. The frottage-treated forest green walls are combined with pale green hand-painted scrolls, resulting in gentle contrast and visible texture.

frottage from the living room to the bath

THIS LIVING ROOM is treated to the frottage technique in shades of blue and taupe that harmonize with the furnishings, window treatments, and accessories. The mottled, uneven finish provides a soft look that's right at home in casual spaces.

THE GRAY GLAZE/PAINT MIXTURE lends a sophisticated feel to this bathroom; the simple black and white accessories keep the focus on the paint treatment, which adds visual interest without overpowering the small space. Small rooms, like this bathroom, may be easier for the beginner to handle than a large room.

project: **frottage** variation

Almost any textural material, including fabric, grass cloth, bamboo shades, or place mats, can be pressed into wet glaze to create an interesting design. In this living room large squares of artist's canvas are pressed into the glaze to create a grid. Dragging a cloth-wrapped finger through the glaze in parallel lines shows the color underneath and creates additional visual excitement.

YOU WILL NEED

- ☐ Satin or semi-gloss latex paint for base coat in desired color
- ☐ Satin or semi-gloss latex paint for top coat in desired color
- ☐ Glaze
- ☐ Painter's tape
- ☐ Bucket and mixing tool
- ☐ Roller and paint tray
- ☐ 16-inch square of unprimed artist's canvas
- ☐ Lint-free cloth

HOW-TO steps

1. Apply the base coat to the surface; let dry.

2. Mix 5 parts glaze to 1 part top coat paint.

3. Roll the glaze/paint mixture onto an approximate 4-foot square section of the wall.

4. Immediately press the unprimed artist's canvas onto the just-glazed section. Lift the canvas off and press onto an adjacent area.
(Photo A)

5. After the entire 4-foot section is textured, wrap the lint-free cloth over your index finger and make groupings of three softly curved—vertical, then horizontal—lines in the wet glaze/paint.
(Photo B)

6. Repeat the process, working in 4-foot sections across the wall.

the **FROTTAGE** technique

■ Frottage, derived from the French term "to rub," *frotter*, can have different looks, depending on the level of contrast between the base and top coats. For a subtle effect, choose two shades of a color. For an exciting, surprising result, use wildly contrasting colors. Experiment with different combinations on a primed sample board to find the right look for your particular project.

YOU WILL NEED

☐ **Satin or semi-gloss latex paint for base coat in desired color**

☐ **Satin or semi-gloss latex paint for top coat in desired color**

☐ **Glaze**

☐ **Bucket and mixing tool**

☐ **Roller and paint tray**

☐ **Newsprint or other paper (i.e., kraft paper or newspaper)**

HOW-TO steps

1. Apply the base coat to the surface; let dry.

2. Mix 5 parts glaze to 1 part top coat paint.

3. Roll the glaze/paint mixture onto an approximate 4-foot square section of the wall.

4. While the top coat mixture is still wet, use both hands to press the newsprint or other paper onto the wall, overlapping and wrinkling it slightly with your hands or a brush.

5. Lift off the paper to remove some of the wet glaze/paint mixture, creating a patterned background. Be careful not to smear the paint as you are removing the paper. (**Photo A**)

6. Repeat the process, continuing to work in approximate 4-foot square sections across the wall. Let each wall dry completely before starting the next to avoid smudging a corner.

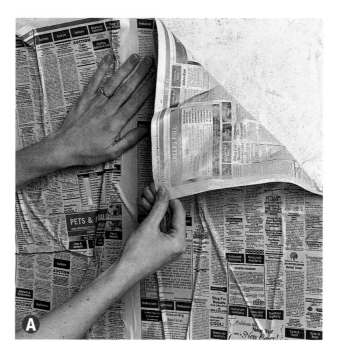

RAGGING

ONE OF THE MOST POPULAR DECORATIVE PAINT TECHNIQUES, ragging—both "positive" and "negative" (see page 65 for more information)—is also one of the easiest to execute on walls and other paintable surfaces like cabinets and furniture.

The basic technique requires the use of a clean, soft, lint-free cotton cloth. Cotton T-shirts are an inexpensive and easy-to-acquire choice, but there are myriad materials, including special ragging mitts, that can be used (see page 65 for examples). To produce the soft look of ragging, you pounce or rub the material on the painted surface; the material can be saturated with a glaze/paint mixture and applied to the wall (positive, or ragging on) or be used dry to remove a glaze/paint mixture from the wall (negative, or ragging off). Whatever material you choose, rotate and refold it often to produce a varied—nonrepetitious—pattern.

Both versions of the technique are appropriate for all room styles, from traditional to contemporary, and look especially pleasing in cottage- and country-style rooms. The colors you choose have a great influence on the type of effect you will get and the style of room it will best suit: Two values of the same color will produce a more subtle, blended look, while dissimilar or contrasting colors will result in wildly dramatic finishes. Regardless of which look you want to achieve, choose colors with care, because the technique can appear busy, especially in small spaces. Be sure to audition the selected colors on a sample board, alternating which is used for the base and top coat to see which look you prefer.

▲ Ragged-on turquoise blue lends a lively kick to this traditional setting.

ragging and stripes

Glazing over ragged stripes gives a hand-painted interpretation of classic, striped wallpaper. Broad, rich alternating stripes of cream and ragged on mocha are the perfect complement to clean white sinks, polished chrome, and a marble tile floor. For information on creating stripes, see page 86.

ragging on and ragging off: what's the difference?

As with many techniques that use glazes, there are both positive and negative application methods. Ragging on is a positive method, in which a glaze/paint mixture is applied to the wall or other surface with a rag. Ragging off is a negative method, in which a glaze/paint mixture is applied to the wall with a brush or roller and then partially removed with a rag.

ragging tool options

Rather than using a cotton cloth, try the following for interesting looks: **A.** Chamois cloth **B.** Ragging mitt **C.** Paper bag **D.** Burlap **E.** Cheesecloth

ragged geometry

CONTRASTING COLORS—in this case olive green and pink—provide a lively, high-energy backdrop for clean white furnishings. The top portion of the wall features the green paint ragged on over a white base coat, while the area within the chair rail moldings showcases a ragged on diamond pattern. Below the chair rail, alternating vertical stripes the same width as the diamonds ground each wall.

For more information on creating diamonds, see page 106; for more information on creating stripes, see page 86.

ragging goes tropical

▲ The reddish-orange walls in this kitchen give the room a warm, tropical feel. Cherry red paint is applied over a bright yellow base coat and ragged off. The green cabinets and purple painted window frame offer cool contrast to the sunny walls.

the RAGGING on and RAGGING off techniques

◼ Ragging on and ragging off require the same materials, and even the same general methods, but when ragging on you will be applying a glaze/paint mixture over a base-coated surface, while in ragging off you will be removing a glaze/paint top coat mixture already applied to the surface.

For either technique, use a soft, lint-free cotton cloth, like a clean T-shirt, or other material (see page 65 for ideas) that is approximately 1 foot square in size. Regardless of which material you choose, keep in mind that the folds in the material produce the pattern, so do not compact the material into a smooth ball; a looser "mound" that can be scrunched easily will produce the most pleasing results.

There are different theories as to whether to use the same cloth or different ones while completing a project. For the most consistent results, use the same cloth, but if it becomes too saturated during the course of the project, it will not hold the glaze/paint mixture as well as you proceed with the project. Clean cloths will accept the glaze/paint mixture better, so if you are going to change cloths during the project, be sure to use the same exact type of material.

When ragging off, you will need to work in sections, similar to many of the other techniques covered in this section. Because you are painting a glaze/paint mixture onto a surface and partially removing it, the working time is limited. Working within an approximate 4-foot square section will allow you the greatest freedom to manipulate the glaze while it is still wet.

When ragging on you do not need to divide the wall into sections, because you will be adding the glaze/paint mixture to the surface and working time is not an issue.

YOU WILL NEED

- ☐ Satin or semi-gloss latex paint for base coat in desired color
- ☐ Satin or semi-gloss latex paint for top coat in desired color
- ☐ Glaze
- ☐ Cotton cloth or other material cut into 1-foot square pieces
- ☐ Bucket and mixing tool
- ☐ Roller or paintbrush and paint tray

TIPS for success

◼ **RAG ROLLING:** To create a more blended look, try using a rolled rag rather than one that has been wadded. Dip the rag into a 4 parts glaze to 1 part paint mixture, twist the rag to roll it into a sausagelike cylinder, and gently roll the rag over the wall.

ragging **on** HOW-TO steps

1. Apply the base coat to the surface; let dry.

2. Mix 4 parts glaze to 1 part top coat paint.

3. Dampen the cloth with water and then wring it out completely (this will help the cloth better accept the glaze/paint mixture). Dip the cloth into the glaze/paint mixture and wring out slightly.

4. Wad up the cloth so that it has an uneven surface. Apply the glaze/paint mixture to the wall, allowing some of the base coat color to show through. Reposition and turn the cloth to avoid repeating the pattern. Use light pressure; too much pressure will result in too much glaze being left on the wall with not enough pattern. (Photo A)

5. Continue reloading the cloth with the glaze/paint mixture and repeat the process until each wall is covered.

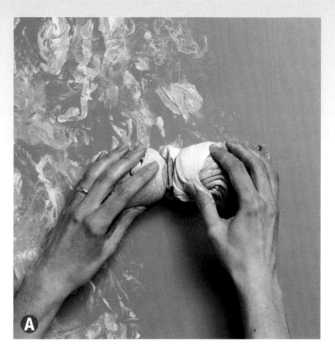

ragging **off** HOW-TO steps

1. Apply the base coat to the surface; let dry.

2. Mix 4 parts glaze to 1 part top coat paint.

3. Apply the paint/glaze mixture onto an approximate 4-foot square section of the wall with a brush or roller.

4. Wad up the cloth so that it has an uneven surface. Press the cloth onto the wall, pouncing and wiping it to remove some of the paint/glaze mixture, exposing some of the base coat. Reposition and turn the rag to avoid repeating the pattern. (Photo B)

5. Repeat the process, continuing to work in approximate 4-foot square sections. Let each wall dry completely before starting the next so you don't smudge a corner.

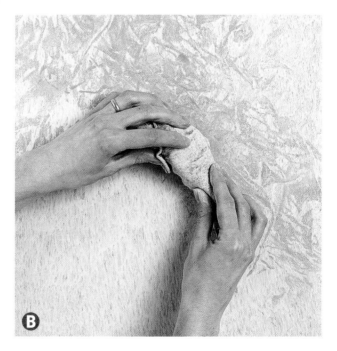

SPONGING

FAST AND EASY TO MASTER, the sponging technique is appropriate in any casual room where you want a soft effect and something more interesting than plain painted walls. The technique entails the use of a damp natural sea sponge to apply paint over a lighter or darker base coat for a mottled, cloudy effect. Sponging can work successfully on any wall surface, including those that are rough or uneven, and can provide a pleasing backdrop for furnishings and artwork in relaxed settings.

Sponge painting has come a long way since its rise to popularity in the 1980s when high-contrast, bold colors were favored. Now more blended, sophisticated looks are preferred for most applications, but experiment with different color combinations on a primed sample board to achieve the effect you desire. For best results, choose two paints that are similar in color (for instance light taupe over dark taupe) or tone (such as medium blue over medium green).

LOW-CONTRAST

MEDIUM-CONTRAST

HIGH-CONTRAST

▲ The casual look of sponged walls makes a perfect backdrop for the salvaged table and country quilt in this cottage-style bedroom. The peach base coat is given more depth with sponged-on cream paint.

▲ Different shades of blue can combine for various effects. These are examples of sponging on.

sponging and stenciling

ALTERNATING SOLID CREAM AND SPONGED-OFF GREEN STRIPES lend distinction to this open foyer, offering guests a warm welcome. A gentle thistle motif is stenciled in the sponged stripes; this adds a final touch of dimension to the walls. See page 134 for more information on stenciling.

Used sparingly, sponging can have dramatic impact in any room.

sponged cabinets

▲ Some of the cabinets in this clean, casual kitchen are given a subtle sponged treatment. Cream paint is sponged on over a light green base coat. The mix of sponged, white painted, and natural wood cabinets adds interest to the space.

sponge options

While a natural sea sponge is the preferred material to use for both sponging techniques, you can also use a sponging mitt or a common household sponge.

A. SEA SPONGE: This type of sponge holds paint well. The irregular size of the pores results in interesting patterns, but you will need to rotate the sponge during the course of a project to avoid a repetitious pattern. Note that pore size affects the final look: Small pores will produce a tight pattern, while large pores will result in a looser pattern. Choose a sponge that is easy to hold and manipulate with one hand.

B. SPONGING MITT: The main advantage of using this specialty tool is that you are able to work with a large surface area, reducing the time needed to complete a project. You will still need to rotate the mitt to vary the pattern.

C. HOUSEHOLD SPONGE: This sponge may be used for some applications, for instance if you are making a bricklike design, but it will leave an unnatural pattern.

sponging simple elegance

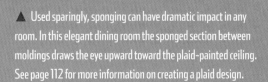

▲ Used sparingly, sponging can have dramatic impact in any room. In this elegant dining room the sponged section between moldings draws the eye upward toward the plaid-painted ceiling. See page 112 for more information on creating a plaid design.

sponged tile

Sponging doesn't have to be limited to walls, furniture, and cabinets: It can add much-needed color and interest to an otherwise plain fireplace surround. Prime the tiles before applying the base coat to the surface.

the SPONGING on and SPONGING off techniques

■ As in ragging, there are both positive (sponging on) and negative (sponging off) techniques. When sponging on you will apply a glaze/paint mixture to a base-coated surface; when sponging off, you will partially remove the glaze/paint mixture just applied in an approximate 4-foot square section (remember, glaze dries quickly, so work in a small area for best results).

For either technique, use a base-coated sample board to experiment with different color combinations. Also, reverse which color is used for the base and top coat. If you are sponging on, you have the opportunity to play with more than one top coat color, although it is recommended to stick to one or two similar colors: Too many colors can result in a dated look.

YOU WILL NEED

☐ **Satin or semi-gloss latex paint for base coat in desired color**

☐ **Satin or semi-gloss latex paint for top coat in desired color**

☐ **Glaze**

☐ **Bucket and mixing tool**

☐ **Roller or paintbrush and paint tray**

☐ **Sea sponge or other sponge applicator**

☐ **Small piece of sponge**

☐ **Paper towels**

☐ **Optional: Cardboard**

HOW-TO steps
sponging on

1. Apply the base coat to the surface; let dry.

2. Mix 4 parts glaze to 1 part top coat paint.

3. Dampen the sea sponge with water and wring thoroughly. Dip the sponge into the glaze/paint mixture, blotting any excess onto paper towels.

4. Lightly press the sponge onto the wall, allowing some of the base coat color to show through. (Photo A) Reposition and turn the sponge to avoid repeating the pattern.

5. Continue reloading the sponge with the glaze/paint mixture and repeat the process until each wall is covered.

6. After sponging each wall, go back and fill in the edges and corners with a smaller piece of sponge. (Photo B) If desired, use cardboard to protect the adjacent walls from being oversponged.

7. Stand back and evaluate your work; fill in any spots that require additional coverage.

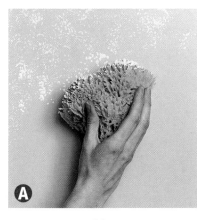

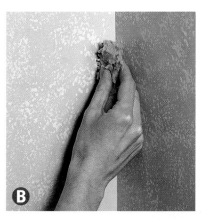

sponging off

1. Apply the base coat to the surface; let dry.

2. Mix 4 parts glaze to 1 part top coat paint.

3. Apply the glaze/paint mixture onto an approximate 4-foot square section of the wall with a paintbrush or roller.

4. Dampen the sea sponge with water and wring thoroughly. Press the sponge onto the just-glazed section of the wall, removing some of the glaze/paint mixture. Rotate the sponge as you work so you don't repeat any pattern. (Photo C) As the sponge becomes saturated with the glaze/paint mixture, blot it on paper towels or wring it out in a bucket.

5. Repeat the process, continuing to work in approximate 4-foot square sections. Let each wall dry completely before starting the next so you don't smudge a corner.

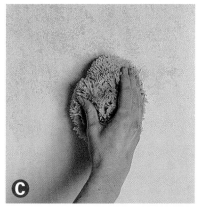

TIPS for success

■ Don't saturate the sponge with paint or use heavy pressure to apply the paint. To avoid a heavy, mottled appearance, dab the glaze/paint mixture on lightly. Repeat if more coverage is needed.

COMBING
Pinstripes, Moiré, and Burlap

COMBS AND SQUEEGEES ARE TWO OF THE MOST VERSATILE TOOLS you can use to create highly textured, dynamic looks. In this section you will see how a comb can be used to make basic pinstripes and moiré patterns and how using both a comb and squeegee can result in a unique burlap pattern. But why stop there? You can create zigzags, random swirls, and even a basket weave design.

For any combing technique, you simply drag a notched comb over a wet glaze/paint top coat mixture, removing some of the top coat to expose the base coat color in one continuous motion. A steady hand is necessary for satisfactory results for any technique that requires a continuous motion. If the thought of undertaking an entire wall is daunting, try working in smaller areas, for instance beneath a chair rail or within square or rectangular sections of molding. (For best results, add the molding after the painting is complete.)

Look to home improvement, crafts, and paint stores for combs to be used for the various techniques highlighted in this section. The most common types are small handheld rubber combs that have notches cut in one or all sides and notched squeegees. See page 81 for information on turning an inexpensive window squeegee into a customized comb. It is best to experiment with each type of comb to see which is most comfortable and has the correctly spaced notches for your particular project.

Each of the techniques featured in this section can work successfully in many types of room settings, but in general consistent pinstripes look best in formal settings, busy moiré in high-energy locations, and more subdued burlap in spaces decorated in formal or country styles. Naturally, color choice has an effect on what the final result will be. Soft shades of color work well in casual settings, while bolder colors suit more contemporary spaces.

ready-made combing tools

Combs come ready made in various shapes and sizes. Stripes of any width can be created with a custom-cut squeegee.

combed custom furniture

DON'T LIMIT COMBING TECHNIQUES TO WALLS. *Sections on furniture pieces, such as the panels of this wardrobe, can be enhanced with patterns, including pinstripes and burlap. These smaller, flat sections may prove to be more manageable, especially if you are trying out the technique for the first time.*

A steady hand is necessary for techniques that require a continuous motion. But relax: A few naturally wavy spots only enhance the hand-painted charm.

wearing **pinstripes** at home

This home office gets a fresh country feel with a combed treatment of salmon over red.

the PINSTRIPE technique

■ The most basic of the combing techniques, defined pinstripes, requires a steady hand for an even pattern. To help guide you as you work, use the last stripe of the just-combed section and start your next combing motion right next to it. If the glaze dries too quickly work in alternating vertical sections, similar to the dragging (strié) technique described on page 49.

YOU WILL NEED

☐ Satin or semi-gloss latex paint for base coat in desired color

☐ Satin or semi-gloss latex paint for top coat in desired color

☐ Glaze

☐ Bucket and mixing tool

☐ Roller and paint tray

☐ Comb or squeegee

HOW-TO steps

1. Apply the base coat to the surface; let dry.

2. Mix 4 parts glaze to 1 part top coat paint.

3. Using a roller, apply the glaze/paint mixture onto an approximate 4-foot wide section of the wall.

4. Holding the comb firmly, carefully drag it down the just-glazed section in one continuous motion. Continue combing down the wall, using the just-combed section as a guide. (**Photo A**)

5. Repeat the process, alternating between rolling and combing in approximate 4-foot wide sections. Let each wall dry completely before starting the next so you don't smudge a corner.

Ⓐ

COMBING**BASICS**

■ Boldly combed stripes may be too much for a whole room, so consider using this technique below a chair rail or within panels.

■ The higher the sheen of the base coat, the more easily the glaze can be manipulated. A satin or semi-gloss paint is ideal for any combing technique.

■ Creating a combed pattern in corners may prove difficult. Solve the problem by either using a multisided comb or creating a pint-size squeegee with the same size notches as the larger version.

■ Because you are taking glaze off of the wall, combing techniques can be quite messy. Be liberal with drop cloths and keep wet rags on hand for quick cleanup.

■ If the comb you are using is too flexible, tape it to a putty knife for easier handling.

■ Working with a partner may create more consistent results: One person can apply the glaze/paint mixture, and the other can begin combing immediately.

moiré your way to a fresh look

A delicate moiré pattern gives this living room a fresh, modern feel. The high-energy pattern imparts a sense of movement, but the cool lavender paint keeps the space relaxed.

the MOIRÉ technique

■ This technique is best accomplished when you work within taped-off sections such as stripes. The high-energy pattern may overwhelm a space if it isn't used sparingly. In the example shown, 8-inch-wide stripes are used.

YOU WILL NEED

- ☐ **Satin or semi-gloss latex paint for base coat in desired color**
- ☐ **Satin or semi-gloss latex paint for top coat in desired color**
- ☐ **Glaze**
- ☐ **Painter's tape**
- ☐ **Bucket and mixing tool**
- ☐ **Roller and paint tray**
- ☐ **Comb or squeegee**
- ☐ **Tape measure and carpenter's level**
- ☐ **Colored pencil (to match paints)**

HOW-TO steps

1. Apply the base coat to the surface; let dry.

2. Determine the width of stripes you would like for your wall. Mark and section off the stripes with painter's tape. (**Photo A**)

3. Mix 4 parts glaze to 1 part top coat paint.

4. Paint one stripe with the glaze/paint mixture. Starting at the top of a stripe, pull the comb down the just-glazed section in repeated, wavy "S" motions. Repeat the motions until the entire stripe has been combed, being careful not to get the mixture on the adjacent stripe. (**Photo B**)

5. Starting at the top of the same stripe, repeat the combing but reverse the "S" motions to create the moiré pattern. When this stripe is complete, peel off the tape.

6. Continue painting and glazing alternating stripes until each wall is complete.

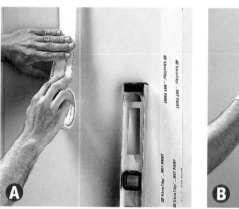

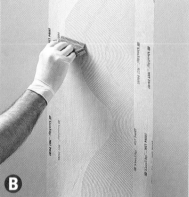

homemade combing tools

Rubber combs are widely available at crafts and specialty paint stores. While some combs are multisided and offer different notch widths on each side, most don't. You can have more control over the size of the pattern by making your own comb with a window-cleaning or screen-painting squeegee. First decide how wide you want the pattern to be. Using a ruler and fine-tip marker, mark the "blade" of the squeegee at the desired widths. Cut out every other notch with a crafts knife.

TIPS for success

■ Combing requires patience and a steady hand. Practice the technique on a primed sample board positioned vertically before tackling a wall.

vintage **burlap**

The burlap technique—shown here in medium and light brown—creates a rustic, neutral backdrop for vintage furniture and natural finishes.

the **BURLAP** technique

■ This technique results in a highly textured finish. While it works very well with traditional burlap colors, such as brown for country-inspired settings, try two shades of gray for a modern, elegant look or black and white for an intense op-art pattern.

YOU WILL NEED

- ☐ Satin or semi-gloss latex paint for base coat in desired color
- ☐ Satin or semi-gloss latex paint for top coat in desired color
- ☐ Glaze
- ☐ Painter's tape
- ☐ Bucket and mixing tool
- ☐ Roller and paint tray
- ☐ Squeegee
- ☐ Fine comb

HOW-TO steps

1. Apply the base coat to the surface; let dry.

2. Divide the room into a series of approximate 2- to 3-foot wide vertical sections. Mask off alternating sections using painter's tape.

3. Mix 4 parts glaze to 1 part top coat paint.

4. Roll the glaze/paint mixture onto one section of the wall. Starting at the top of the just-glazed section pull the squeegee down the wall to make vertical stripes. (Photo A) Quickly repeat the process, using the edge of the previous squeegee stroke as a guide until the entire glazed section is striped.

5. Repeat the process for every masked-off (alternating) section. Let the paint dry at least 6 hours.

6. Leaving the tape in place, paint one section with the glaze/paint mixture (covering the vertical striping). (Photo B) Starting at the top of the section, pull the fine comb horizontally through the glaze. Quickly repeat across the entire glazed section. (Photo C)

7. Continue the horizontal striping process for every masked-off (alternating) section. Remove the tape; let the paint dry.

8. Mask off each unpainted section. Apply the glaze/paint mixture and vertically stripe each remaining section in the same manner as described in Steps 4 and 5. Again allow the paint to dry at least 6 hours.

9. Repeat Steps 6 and 7 until all sections have been horizontally striped. Remove the tape; let the paint dry.

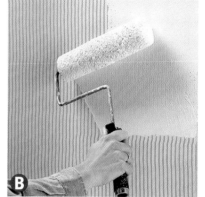

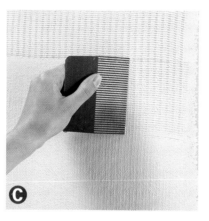

TIPS for success

■ It is easier to **comb out of a corner** than into it, so plan accordingly when you reach corners.

ALL

in GOOD Measure

DO YOU REMEMBER sitting in geometry as a kid thinking, "When am I ever going to use this stuff?" If you are dreaming of a **fun checkerboard floor or romantic diamonds** for bedroom walls, dust off that calculator, grab a pencil, and put that straightedge to use. With a little planning **you can create about any geometric design or pattern imaginable.** On the following pages you will learn how to measure and mark designs like a pro and how combining these geometric designs with such techniques as colorwashing and sponging creates **one-of-a-kind interiors.**

STRIPES

STRIPES ARE THE BUILDING BLOCKS OF THE OTHER TECHNIQUES—GRIDS, DIAMONDS, AND PLAIDS—presented in this section. Once you have mastered the measuring and marking of striped designs, you will easily be able to transition into other more involved techniques. But while stripes are the most basic of the geometric patterns, they certainly aren't boring: They add interest to a room without being too busy and are at home in a space decorated in any manner. Stripes can be created in a variety of widths and color combinations; and by incorporating ragging, colorwashing, stenciling, or other paint techniques, you can take them to another level.

First things first: When you plan to stripe a wall, make sure you measure carefully. If you paint only one bold focal point wall, find a number that divides equally into the width (for vertical stripes) or height (for horizontal stripes) of the wall. If, however, you plan to paint more than one wall, you have two options: You can either find a number

▲ The lighthearted look of this bedroom is achieved with pretty hand-painted stripes in green, yellow, pink, and brown that imitate shirting fabric that's been washed several times. ▶

Fresh shades of green graduate from dark to light in the freely painted, uneven edges of the stripes flowing around this dining room. The 14-inch-wide stripes were not taped off; the stripes were lightly marked and then the five hues were rolled freehand for an uneven transition from one to another.

that divides equally into all of the walls to be painted so that the repeated pattern will begin and end on each wall or have the stripes flow around corners, providing a smooth transition from wall to wall.

When choosing widths for stripes, select what appeals to you, keeping in mind the size of your room and the time you want to dedicate to measuring, marking, and painting. For instance, thin pinstripes on all walls of a large room will be time-consuming from start to finish, so you might want to opt for wider stripes that require less involvement.

Color has a big effect on the resulting look. Narrow pinstripes tend to have a more formal appearance in rich colors like brown and black, but use red and white and you'll have a charming country look. Overall, stripes can be bold, dramatic, or even youthful when completed in vivid or contrasting colors, or mellow and subdued in softer colors, for instance those near each other on a paint card. And remember to think about how paint finish will affect the design: Painting alternating stripes of semi-gloss and flat paint will give your walls an interesting visual texture contrast.

measuring and marking **geometric designs**

■ Whether you want to design simple stripes or create more elaborate plaid or diamond designs, learning how to measure and mark designs correctly will make the process more enjoyable—and save you lots of headaches.

first things first

Before doing anything else, measure the height and width of each wall to be painted with a geometric pattern. Decide the height and/or width of the design desired. Try to find a number that divides evenly into the wall measurements if you want the design to be of equal size—ensuring your pattern won't result in two adjoining sections of the same color—but don't be afraid to let the pattern flow around corners: Measure into the corner of a wall and continue the measurement onto the adjoining wall, starting from the corner. Next use graph paper and a pencil to map out your design. This will allow you to better visualize your design before tackling the actual wall. And it is always wise to create a sample board with the design drawn to scale and painted with the actual solid color or

▲ These tools help ensure satisfactory results for any paint project that incorporates geometric designs.

Ⓐ
▲ Work with a partner to snap accurate chalk lines.

Ⓑ
▲ This combination level/ruler makes measuring and marking easy.

▲ Use colored pencils in the same color as you will be painting for nearly invisible lines.

decorative technique to ensure you like the results before putting time and energy into the project.

tools of the trade

After you have decided on the size and scale of your design, you need to begin measuring the wall (see the individual techniques for specific measuring information). You can use whatever measuring tool suits you, but tape measures, yardsticks, and chalk lines are the most common devices. Chalk lines give you the ability to mark perfect lines for the creation of stripe, block, diamond, or plaid patterns. This

useful tool is a box that contains string on a reel and chalk that is left on the wall when the string is "snapped" on the surface. Snapping chalk lines is best accomplished by two people. (Photo A) After taping you can wipe away the chalk lines. Regardless of which tool you choose, use a carpenter's level to ensure even, straight lines; those with printed measurements are recommended. (Photo B)

mark with colored pencils

Rather than using a regular lead pencil for marking designs on a wall, select colored pencils in shades that match the paint colors you intend to use for the design. By doing so, stray marks will not be noticeable. You can use a different colored pencil for each color portion of the design to help you visualize your plan. Use colored pencils for both marking and joining the lines of a design. (Photo C) Colored pencil marks that are not painted over may easily be cleaned with dishsoap and a washcloth.

to tape or not to tape

After you have marked your design, you need to decide whether you want a crisp, clean pattern or a looser, freer pattern. For crisp lines, use painter's tape to mask off the areas to be painted. Tape inside the lines of the sections not being painted so that the paint comes right up to the line that divides the pattern. (Photo D) When you are finished painting one color, immediately remove the tape; let dry. Retape and continue the process until your design is complete. For looser lines, use the colored pencil or chalk lines to guide you. For better control use a small artist's brush to hand-paint designs.

Regardless of whether or not you choose to tape, mark those areas not to be painted with pieces of painter's tape. (Photo E) This way you will eliminate the chance of painting a portion of the design with the wrong color, which could be disastrous, especially when painting an alternating pattern.

C

▲ Join the marks with a colored pencil; use a level for perfectly straight lines.

D

▲ If you want crisp lines, tape just to the left or right of the lines drawn with the colored pencil; for a looser look, simply use the lines as a guide for hand painting.

E

▲ If you are painting alternating sections, it is helpful to put an "X" with tape in the areas not to be painted.

striping possibilities

▲ Bold stripes in gold and silver metallic paint transform a 1920s-era chest into a spirited yet traditional accent. The unconventional paint colors emphasize the delicately turned legs on this period piece.

▲ A uniform, double-stripe pattern doesn't have to feel stuffy: When painted freehand over marked lines, it has a looser look. A highly reflective metallic copper acrylic paint is used on this wall.

▲ The bold 8-inch-wide stripes in this farmhouse-style girl's room ground the room without being boring. Light aqua serves as the base coat, and darker aqua paint is used on alternating stripes.

▲ Complementary bands of copper paint and two shades of green make fine companions in this bedroom: The tones are similar so they don't overwhelm, and the white moldings frame the pattern well. The uneven stripes—6, 12, 18, and 30 inches wide—are an interesting take on a fun pattern.

stripes are always welcome

◄ Well-planned and careful taping can produce crisp stripes, as shown in this porch floor "runner." By painting only a narrow runner in front of the door instead of extending the pattern across the entire floor, attention is called to the house's entry. Crisp green and white are used on this porch, but you can create an equally attractive look with shades similar to those used in summery striped outdoor fabrics.

thinking about scale

■ Stripes, both vertical and horizontal, can be a dramatic backdrop for rooms decorated in all styles. Before you start measuring, marking, and painting, think about how the stripes will interact with furnishings and accessories in the room. To design stripes around furnishings, position the furniture where you want it and measure stripes up from there. In the room *right* the stripes are a distinctive backdrop above the shelving unit, eliminating the need for artwork.

▶ For a fresh, contemporary look, turn traditional stripes on their sides. Painting horizontal stripes of multiple colors brings eye-catching style to monochromatic walls. Crisp, cool blue stripes add depth and weight to the walls in this living room.

project: painted floorcloth

■ Bring pattern and color to a bare floor with an inexpensive painted floorcloth. Floorcloths like the one shown here are most often made of nonfraying preprimed canvas that has been painted with artist's gesso or interior latex wall primer. Available in art supply stores, canvas is sold by the ounce, per square foot, or by a number and name; the higher the number the stronger the canvas. Also look for preprimed canvas already cut into shapes, such as ovals and circles, at crafts stores.

YOU WILL NEED

- ☐ Yardstick or tape measure
- ☐ Colored pencils, in colors to match border and stripe paint colors
- ☐ 1-inch-wide painter's tape
- ☐ 3-inch paint rollers and paint tray
- ☐ Paper plate
- ☐ Scrap of cardboard
- ☐ Scissors
- ☐ 4x5-foot preprimed canvas
- ☐ Acrylic paint in three desired colors
- ☐ Flat-finish acrylic polyurethane and paintbrush

HOW-TO steps

1. Measure a 6-inch border all around the perimeter of the preprimed canvas; mark lightly with a colored pencil.

2. Adhere the painter's tape to the canvas along the pencil marks, pressing firmly for a crisp edge.

3. In the center of the canvas, measure and mark alternating 5- and 3-inch-wide stripes with a colored pencil, extending the lines to the taped-off border area. Tape along each line, pressing firmly.

4. Pour one color of paint into the paint tray. Dip a 3-inch roller into the paint and blot excess paint on the tray ramp. Roll the paint on the 5-inch-wide stripes; let dry. Repeat with another color of paint, applying the paint to the narrow 1-inch-wide stripes with another roller; let dry. Paint the border area with the remaining paint color; let dry.

Note: The floorcloth above has unpainted 1-inch-wide stripes on either side of the narrow painted stripes.

5. Carefully remove all of the tape.

6. With the pencil and paper plate, trace a half-circle onto the scrap of cardboard for the border template. Cut out.

7. Starting in the center of each side of the canvas, trace the half-circle onto the border several times, stopping short of the corner. Draw the corner scallops freehand to connect adjoining sides. Cut out the scalloped border.

8. Apply two coats of polyurethane to the entire canvas, letting it dry thoroughly between coats.

the STRIPING technique

■ Even though stripes require careful measuring to ensure satisfactory results, you will discover the process is really quite easy—and addictive—once you get the hang of it. Remember that you can choose any width desired for your striped design, even selecting stripes of different widths. After you've determined the width of the stripes, there are still some other factors to consider: You need to select a pleasing color palette of two or three colors that achieves the look you desire, may select a technique to apply to the stripes (such as colorwashing), and decide whether you want crisp, perfectly straight or looser, hand-painted stripes.

YOU WILL NEED

☐ Optional: Latex paint for base coat in desired color and finish

☐ Latex paint for top coat in desired color(s) and finish

☐ Painter's tape

☐ Roller or paintbrush and paint tray

☐ Colored pencils (to match paints)

☐ Tape measure

☐ Yardstick

☐ Carpenter's level

☐ Chalk line

HOW-TO steps

1. If desired apply a base coat to the wall in the lightest desired stripe color.

2. Measure the width of each wall to be painted for vertical stripes or the height of each wall for horizontal stripes. Decide what width you want the stripes to be. Try to find a number that divides evenly into the wall measurements if you want the stripes to be equal sizes.

3. Using a colored pencil and tape measure or yardstick, mark the wall at the ceiling and floor, as well as points between to ensure straight lines. Join the marks with the yardstick and a colored pencil, using a level to ensure accurate, even lines. If desired you can use a chalk line for this process.

4. For crisp stripes use painter's tape to mask off the stripes of one color: Tape an "X" inside the lines drawn for each stripe not being painted at this time (see page 89). Paint the stripes, remove the tape, and let dry. Repeat the taping and painting process for each color(s).

5. For a casual, looser appearance, do not use painter's tape to mask off the striped sections; simply use the colored pencil or chalk lines as guides and paint the stripes.

▲ **Equal-width stripes**

▲ **Random-width stripes**

▲ **Equal-width stripes divided by thin sashings**

BLOCKS, CHECKS, and GRIDS

IT'S COOL TO BE SQUARE. Blocks of color brushed right onto a wall is an easy way to lift any room above the ordinary and introduce a few—or a whole palette—of your favorite hues. Like stripes, you can use solid colors or introduce techniques such as colorwashing or sponging to achieve a variety of looks. While stripes can be used in rooms decorated in nearly any style, blocks are best reserved for casual spaces. Furthermore blocks may tend to get overwhelming, so limit the technique to high-ceilinged larger rooms that won't be overpowered by the pattern or design one focal-point wall in a room and paint the other walls in one color or technique used on the patterned wall.

▲ Blocks increase in size as they move down this 8-foot-tall wall. A row of 46-inch-tall blocks along the bottom anchors the design. The blocks are created with layered gold, pale yellow, cream, and scarlet glazes. See page 28 for more information on glazing techniques.

▲ Basic block pattern

▲ Basic check pattern

▲ Basic grid pattern

defining **blocks, checks,** and **grids**

In this book, these terms distinguish the different square patterns from one another.

■ **blocks** are squares that butt up against one another and are painted in more than two colors in a repeated or random pattern.

■ **checks** are squares that also butt up against one another, but only two colors are used in a repeated pattern.

■ **grids** are squares that are divided by sashings, thin lines that run vertically and horizontally between the squares. Grids can be made up of two or more colors in a repeated or random pattern.

painting a subfloor

■ When your finances and taste level don't match up, you may need to call on extreme but temporary measures. One way to deal with badly worn, stained, or otherwise unsalvageable carpet may be to remove it and paint the solid subfloor. Because floor paint dries harder than wall paint, it stands up to the wear and tear a walking surface normally takes.

Use this technique on sturdy subfloors such as plywood and particleboard, not plank-style hardwood flooring. Remove the old carpet and scrape away any remaining adhesive or residue. Fill in gouges, gaps, indentations, and cracks with wood fill. If large gaps remain between the boards, try to work the pattern around them, making the cracks fall at the design's edges. Sand the surface smooth, wipe it clean, and prime. Paint the entire floor one base coat color, then add the design.

When choosing colors for a geometric seating-area pattern such as this, use related hues, but vary the width and color placement for interest. If the paint is in an area where furniture routinely slides across the floor, add a top coat of floor-grade polyurethane. On most floors, though, the paint alone is durable enough.

high- or low-contrast **blocks**

▲ High-contrast color combinations—such as the greens, browns, and purples shown in this living room—look cutting edge and contemporary.

▲ Uniform squares as shown in this bedroom create a sense of movement, even when they are interrupted by such details as windows. Soft yellow, celery green, purple, and taupe blocks provide a soothing backdrop in this bedroom.

the **bowtie block** design

The walls of this playroom come alive with the energy of blocks painted in bold colors. Black squares set on-point create the bowtie design.

■ IF YOU LOVE BLOCKS AND GRIDS but are looking for an interesting twist, try a bowtie design. First mark and paint the large block or checkerboard pattern; let dry. Then measure and mark a smaller square—essentially a diamond—that will cover the join of four blocks to form the bowtie.

Periwinkle blue paint and natural wood checks on the floor of this cottage-style bedroom add enduring style. The bowtie is created with combed squares in a very pale blue at the join of the large squares. The large pattern creates a strong anchor for the room and mixes successfully with the grid pattern on the quilt and small floral-motif window treatments. See page 76 for more information on combing.

teen green and white **checks**

▲ Green and white checks pop off the walls in this teenage girl's room. From a distance, the checks look very precise; however, on closer inspection you can see that each check is slightly uneven. This loose hand-painted treatment is fresh and relaxed, making it the perfect backdrop for whimsical artwork and lively fabrics on the loveseat and table. The pink dots add a playful element to the walls.

checks for breakfast

▲ Four-inch-square green and white checks give character to the lower portion of the walls in this cute cottage kitchen. As a whimsical touch, 2x1¹/₂-inch-wide stripes are hand-painted above the checks as a border. The same green used on the walls freshens the kitchen cabinets, while simple white stools are hand-painted with floral motifs. See page 122 for more information on hand painting.

the bathroom is a **peach**

▲ The walls of this bathroom have a pale peach base coat. Varying layers of yellow, teal, and peach glaze achieve a watery, translucent look within the block design. See page 28 for information on glazing techniques.

pink and white **checks**

▲ Funky designs and cheery pastel colors brighten this young girl's room. The bed's headboard and footboard, as well as the wardrobe, are brought to life with a pink and white checked design and hand-painted embellishments, including vines, polka dots, and smaller checks. While the walls appear as though they have been hand-painted, they are in fact covered with diamond-pattern wallpaper. A simple hand-painted wavy border accented with polka dots flows across the top of each wall. For more information on hand painting, see page 122.

project: **checkerboard** dresser

A notched squeegee becomes a magic wand when it is used to update an otherwise plain dresser. For more information on combing techniques, see page 76; to learn how to make a comb from a squeegee, see page 81.

YOU WILL NEED

- ☐ **Unfinished dresser**
- ☐ **Primer**
- ☐ **Semi-gloss paint in two colors**
- ☐ **Glaze**
- ☐ **Painter's tape**
- ☐ **Bucket and mixing tool**
- ☐ **Paintbrushes, 3-inch roller, and paint tray**
- ☐ **Squeegee with ¼-inch notches**
- ☐ **Lint-free cloth**
- ☐ **Acrylic polyurethane sealer**
- ☐ **Screwdriver**

HOW-TO steps

1. Remove knobs from the drawers, if necessary. Apply primer to the dresser, drawers, and knobs; let dry.

2. Apply one color of paint to the entire dresser and drawer fronts; let dry.

3. Tape off the edges of each drawer front, pressing firmly for a crisp edge. **(Photo A)**

4. Mix 1 part of the remaining color of paint to 1 part glaze. With the 3-inch roller, apply the glaze/paint mixture to one drawer front. **(Photo B)**

5. Immediately pull the notched squeegee vertically down the drawer front to remove some of the glaze/paint mixture. Continue combing in a vertical direction until the entire drawer front has been combed. Wipe the squeegee with the lint-free cloth, then drag the squeegee horizontally across the drawer to make a checked pattern. **(Photo C)** Wipe the squeegee clean. Continue to paint and squeegee the drawer fronts, one at a time. Let all dry.

6. Paint the drawer knobs as desired; let dry. Screw the knobs to the drawers.

7. Apply two coats of polyurethane to the dresser and drawer fronts; let dry between coats.

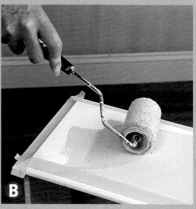

B

A

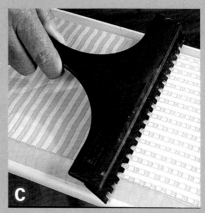

C

rectangles of interest

▲ Who says geometric shapes have to be all of the same size to be effective? Two large rectangles, one vertical and one horizontal, and a series of smaller rectangles bring architectural interest to this living room. Choosing the paint colors in a room like this is simple: Select four colors from one paint strip, using the darkest color for the overall background and consecutively lighter colors for the elements in the foreground. A treatment such as this creates an exciting focal point in a room with minimal furnishings, which allows the wall treatment to take center stage.

great gingham look

THE GINGHAM DESIGN—which uses layered stripes of paint to imitate the look of woven fabric—is a variation of the checks technique. In this example, light blue vertical and horizontal stripes are painted over a white base coat, then the intersecting squares are filled in with a slightly deeper blue to add definition to the design.

▲ **Basic gingham pattern**

the BLOCKS, CHECKS, and GRIDS techniques

■ Whether you choose multicolor blocks, playful checks, or a bold grid, making squares is an easy way to say goodbye to boring walls. As with stripes careful planning and measuring are required for best results, but the designs give you the ability to incorporate a rainbow of colors if desired. For exact, crisp lines, use painter's tape to mask off the squares as you paint; otherwise, use colored pencil or chalk lines as a guide for less formal, hand-painted squares.

If you are designing a grid, keep in mind that you will need to allow for the sashings. For instance, if you want 22-inch squares with a 1-inch sash between, you will need to figure it into your planning and measuring; see page 95 for more information. One trick that may help you save time is purchasing painter's tape in the width desired for the sashings. You can keep this tape in place while you paint all of the blocks so you are not constantly taping and retaping throughout the process.

YOU WILL NEED

- ☐ Optional: Latex paint for base coat in desired color and finish
- ☐ Latex paint for top coat in desired color(s) and finish
- ☐ Painter's tape
- ☐ Roller or paintbrush and paint tray
- ☐ Colored pencils (to match paints)
- ☐ Tape measure
- ☐ Yardstick
- ☐ Carpenter's level
- ☐ Chalk line

block, check, and grid patterns at a glance

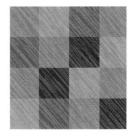

▲ Basic block pattern

▲ Basic check pattern

▲ Basic grid pattern

▲ Basic gingham pattern

HOW-TO steps

1. If desired apply a base coat to the wall in one of the desired colors. If you are creating a grid design, use the base coat as the sashing color.

2. Measure the height and width of the wall to be painted. Decide what size you want the squares to be, with or without sashings. Try to find a number that divides evenly into the wall measurements if you want the squares to be equal sizes. If the wall can't be divided into equal sizes, begin the design at the ceiling and move down; let it run out at the floor, where a smaller design will be less noticeable.

3. Use a colored pencil and tape measure or yardstick to mark the wall at the ceiling and floor, as well as points between, to ensure straight lines at the desired widths for the vertical portions of the squares. Join the marks with a colored pencil

and a level to ensure accurate, even lines. If desired you can also snap a chalk line for this process. Repeat this process by making marks along the wall at the desired heights for the horizontal portions of the squares.

4. For crisp squares use painter's tape to mask off the squares of one color: Tape an "X" inside the lines drawn for each square not being painted at this time (see page 89). Paint the remaining squares, remove the tape, and let dry. Repeat the taping and painting process with the remaining color(s), until the entire wall is covered.

5. For a casual, looser appearance, do not use painter's tape to mask off the square sections; simply use the colored pencil or chalk lines as guides and paint the squares.

DIAMONDS

WHETHER THEY ARE IN THE ROMANTIC HARLEQUIN STYLE or simply squares set on-point, diamonds are a classy addition to nearly any room: Large black and white diamonds look crisp and tailored for formal settings, hand-painted diamonds in bright, cheerful colors are perfect for children's rooms, and earth tones can be used effectively for rooms decorated with casual or country furnishings and accessories.

Like other visually "busy" techniques such as bold blocks, you may want to consider using an allover diamond pattern only on a focal-point wall; paint the other walls with a solid color or use a technique featured in the diamond design, such as colorwashing, sponging, or any of the texture-rich techniques featured in Section 1. If you want diamonds on all of the walls of a room, consider one flowing row that runs around the room.

If you want to incorporate the drama of diamonds in a room, walls aren't the only option: Look to the floor.

▲ Hand-painted, colorwashed harlequin diamonds in seven different shades of green make a serene and elegant backdrop for an oil painting and traditional furnishings and accessories. The adjoining walls of this living room are painted in a soft green colorwash that both complements and keeps the focus on the patterned wall. The diagonal lines of a diamond pattern break up boxy spaces, as in this room. See page 32 for more information on colorwashing.

floored over **diamonds**

▲ Don't limit dramatic paint treatments to the rooms inside your home: Porches, decks, and patios can benefit from them too. This inviting porch has green and white diamonds on its floor.

▲ A white floor is given a dramatic look with a blue diamond grid. Gold mariner's compasses stenciled at random over some of the grid intersections give additional interest. The simple furnishings and window treatments in this room put the focus on the floor. See page 134 for more information on stenciling.

This strong design element can visually anchor a room—especially when one of the colors featured is also used on the walls—and give much-needed pattern punch. Diamond patterns are a great way to visually widen a long, narrow hallway because diagonal lines are the longest lines through a space. The most common approach is to use a checkerboard pattern, with white, off-white, or stained wood alternating with a color. Regardless of the colors or the scale of the pattern chosen, make sure the window and wall treatments are simple and don't compete with the floor for attention. Regardless if you are painting a diamond pattern or other technique on a floor, treat the floor with a floor-grade polyurethane to stand up to normal wear unless you are using a specially formulated floor paint.

stenciled **diamonds**

◆ If measuring and marking walls sounds too time-intensive, create a personalized stencil to make the job easier. First draw a diamond in the size desired on a piece of cardstock. Trace the diamond onto stencil plastic; repeat to make a vertical row. Cut out every other diamond with a crafts knife. Determine how much wall you want to cover. Mark off that section using a carpenter's level and pencil. Paint the section the lightest color in the design; let dry. Position the stencil in a corner or on the edge of the wall; secure with tape or stencil adhesive. Paint alternating diamonds with the desired color; repeat across the wall and let dry. See page 134 for more information on stenciling.

diamonds overhead

◄ Three equal-size squares, set on-point to appear as diamonds, bring attention to this ceiling. To achieve this look, mask off the outer 1½ inches with painter's tape to form borders, then paint the diamonds with a green base coat. After the base coat is dry, apply a metallic glaze with a wallpaper brush to create a strié effect. Mask the borders and paint them a coordinating color. This ceiling treatment works well in narrow rooms with a smooth ceiling surface. See page 46 for more information on strié (dragging).

diamonds set on-point

DIAMONDS DON'T HAVE TO BE TALLER THAN THEY ARE WIDE: This technique involves setting squares on-point, or at a 45-degree angle, to appear as diamonds. This variation of the basic checks pattern (see page 95) works especially well on floors.

To achieve this look, follow the instructions for the classic harlequin diamond on page 111, but measure and mark points that are the same height and width, as in the diagram shown *right*.

▲ Diamonds set on-point pattern

diamonds for dining

◀ Solid-color and sponged diamonds bring status to this once-unadorned tabletop. A solid ½-inch border around the diamonds sets off the pattern, made up of three colors, which alternate between solid and sponged. To protect a painted tabletop apply two coats of clear water-base polyurethane. See page 70 for more information on sponging.

diamonds bright and bold

▶ The diamond pattern on the lower third of these walls breathes new life into an old-fashioned bathroom. Watermelon pink, apple green, and banana yellow are combined in this fun treatment. Style also comes from a hand-painted "wave" border on the wall and floorcloth and layers of watermelon pink glaze on the top portion of the wall. For more information on hand-painted motifs, see page 122; for information on creating floorcloths, see page 92; and for information on layering glazes, see page 28. ▼

sweet **diamond** dreams

▲ Large-scale, hand-painted diamonds in a repeated row are perfect for romantic settings, as in this bedroom. The three diamonds run the width of the bed, creating the look of a headboard and giving the treatment focal-point status.

the harlequin **DIAMONDS** technique

■ This classic design with diamonds that are taller than they are wide is very versatile: Large or small diamond patterns lend a sophisticated feel to rooms decorated in any manner; use color to capture the look you are after.

When planning your diamond design, keep the scale of the room and its furnishings in mind. And remember the smaller the pattern the more time-consuming the process will be, because you will need to measure, mark, and paint more diamonds.

Follow the steps below if you are working alone, but if you work with a partner, use a chalk line to its full extent: Mark points around the perimeter of the wall and connect with the chalk line.

YOU WILL NEED

- ☐ Optional: Latex paint for base coat in desired color and finish
- ☐ Latex paint for top coat in desired color(s) and finish
- ☐ Painter's tape
- ☐ Roller or paintbrush and paint tray
- ☐ Colored pencils (to match paints)
- ☐ Tape measure
- ☐ Yardstick
- ☐ Carpenter's level
- ☐ Optional: Chalk line
- ☐ Graph paper

HOW-TO steps

1. If desired apply a base coat to the wall in the lightest desired color.

2. Measure the wall to be painted and choose the size and scale of the diamonds. Using graph paper draw out the desired diamond design. (In the design shown *below right*, the diamonds are 6 inches tall and 4 inches wide.)

3. Starting at an upper corner of the wall, where it meets the ceiling, measure half of the width of the diamond design (in our example 2 inches) and make a mark with a colored pencil. After that mark, measure the full width of the diamond design (in our example 4 inches) across the wall until you reach the end.

4. Return to the first mark made in Step 3. Measure down from this mark the height of the diamond (in our example 6 inches); make a mark here. Continue across the wall, using the marks made in Step 3 as a guide, until you reach the end.

5. Using the first mark made in Step 4, continue measuring and marking the height of the diamond until the entire wall is marked. The height of each diamond has now been measured.

6. To measure and mark the width of each diamond, return to the first mark made in Step 3. Measure down half of the height of the diamond (in this case 3 inches) and then across half of the width of the diamond (in our example 2 inches). Make a mark here. After that mark, measure the full width of the diamond design across the wall until you reach the end.

7. Using the first mark made in Step 6, continue measuring and marking the width of the diamond until the entire wall is marked. The width of each diamond has now been measured.

8. When you are done measuring and marking the entire wall, diagonally connect the lines with a colored pencil and yardstick, creating the diamond design.

9. For crisp diamonds, use painter's tape to mask off the lines and tape an "X" within each diamond not to be painted (for example alternating diamonds in the design); see page 89. Paint the diamonds with the top coat paint; remove the tape and let dry.

10. For a casual, looser appearance, do not use painter's tape to mask off the diamonds; simply use the colored pencil or chalk lines as guides and paint the diamonds with the top coat paint.

4"
3"
6"
2"

Measure and mark as described in steps if working alone.

Mark points around perimeter of wall and snap with chalk line if working with a partner.

▲ **Harlequin diamonds pattern**

PLAIDS

ONE OF THE MOST IMPRESSIVE of all the techniques covered in this book, plaid is also one of the most difficult to execute. Not only do you have to map out your design carefully before beginning, but you also have to select your palette with care—and painting multiple colors means you have to dedicate additional time to preparation, drying time, and cleanup. Regardless, if you have a room that needs some punch, plaid is a great choice. And if you limit it to smaller rooms, use the design on one focal-point wall, or paint plaid accents on a furniture piece, it will be less time-consuming and still have impact.

For the traditional plaid design, which is explained on page 115, you will measure and paint the larger plaid design over a background color. Then the thinner lines are added over the larger portion of the design, creating a multilayer stripe pattern. Continuity is a key to this design: It is easiest to paint plaid on walls that have no window or door openings or other interruptions.

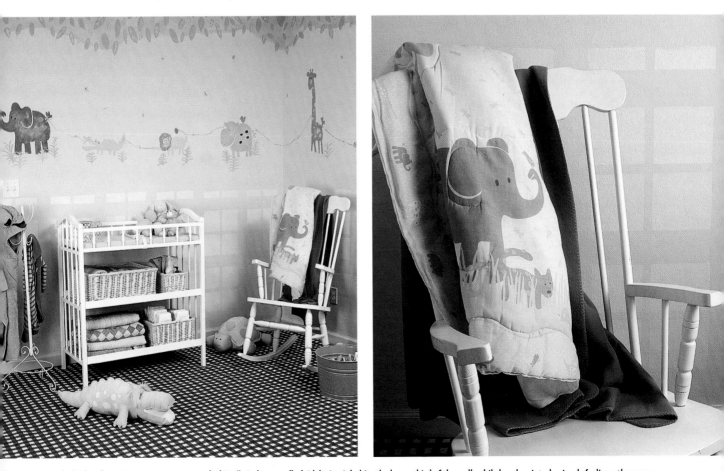

▲ In this charming nursery, a green and white "windowpane" plaid design inhabits the lower third of the wall, while hand-painted animals frolic on the space above. This simple design is created in two colors, which is easier to paint than multicolor patterns. See page 122 for more information on hand-painted motifs.

simply mad about **plaid**

◀ Mad about plaid but leery of painting an entire wall? Furniture pieces with simple lines, such as this sideboard, are a great starting point for this technique. Three hues of paint mingle with stained wood on the drawer fronts and top of this piece in a random-width plaid design.

▶ An area "rug" painted right on the floor in a plaid pattern creates a bright, jazzy welcome to all who dine in this kitchen. The stripes that create the plaid design are based on one measurement, 3½ inches, that's multiplied by two or three. This base measurement nets a finished design with an overall measurement of 105x140 inches. Some of the lines are the result of applying paint with the edge of a household sponge. See page 70 for more information on sponging.

dine in casual **plaid**

▲ Blue and taupe combine for a loose, casual, hand-painted plaid design in this dining room. The solid blue paint beneath the chair rail grounds the design.

the **PLAIDS** technique

■ Plaid is a fun way to incorporate different colors into your decorating scheme. For this basic technique, use four colors, one for the background and three for the stripes. Don't be afraid to alter the basic pattern provided: By leaving additional space between the stripes, the background color will be more visible and the stripes will have more impact.

YOU WILL NEED

☐ **Latex paint for base coat in desired color and finish**

☐ **Latex paint for top coat in desired colors and finish**

☐ **Painter's tape**

☐ **Roller or paintbrush and paint tray**

☐ **Colored pencils (to match paints)**

☐ **Tape measure**

☐ **Yardstick**

☐ **Carpenter's level**

☐ **Chalk line**

☐ **Graph paper**

HOW-TO steps

1. Apply the base coat to the wall in the lightest desired color.

2. Measure the width of each wall to be painted for vertical stripes, and the height of the wall for horizontal stripes. Decide what width you want the large stripes to be (in the design shown *right*, the large stripes are 4 inches wide, with 5 inches between to allow for two 1-inch-wide stripes in different colors with the base coat visible between). Try to find a number that divides evenly into the wall measurements.

3. Using graph paper draw out the desired plaid design. Measure and mark the vertical lines of the widest part of the design using the colored pencils. Mark the wall at the ceiling and floor, as well as points between to ensure accurate, even stripes. Use the level to extend the marks and make vertical lines from the top to the bottom of the wall. You can also snap a chalk line for this process.

4. For crisp stripes use painter's tape to mask off the vertical lines and tape an "X" within each area not to be painted (see page 89). Paint the vertical lines within the painter's tape with one color of top coat paint; remove the tape and let dry.

5. For a casual, looser appearance, do not use painter's tape to mask off the lines; simply use the colored pencil or chalk lines as guides and paint the large stripes.

6. Using the same measurement as in Step 3, mark the wide horizontal lines as you did the vertical, masking of the lines with tape, if desired. Paint the horizontal stripes; let dry.

7. Draw the vertical and horizontal lines for the narrower (in this case 1-inch-wide) sections of the plaid design on top of the larger design just painted. If desired, use painter's tape to mask off the areas to be painted following Steps 2 through 6. Paint the vertical and horizontal lines of one color; remove tape if necessary and let dry. Repeat the process with the remaining vertical and horizontal lines and final paint color.

▼ **The basic plaid pattern**

▲ Plaid can take on different looks depending on the color combination used and whether the design is loosely hand-painted or crisply taped.

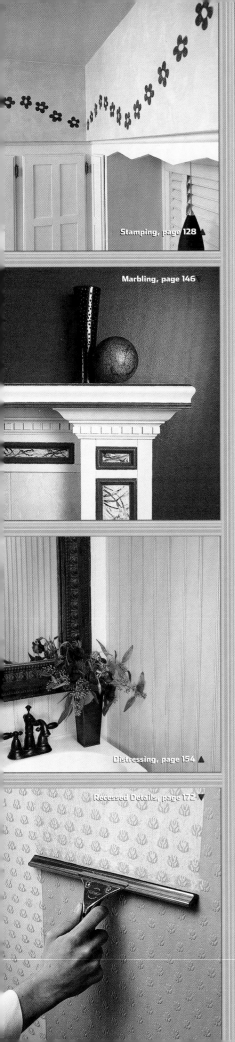

TECHNIQUE

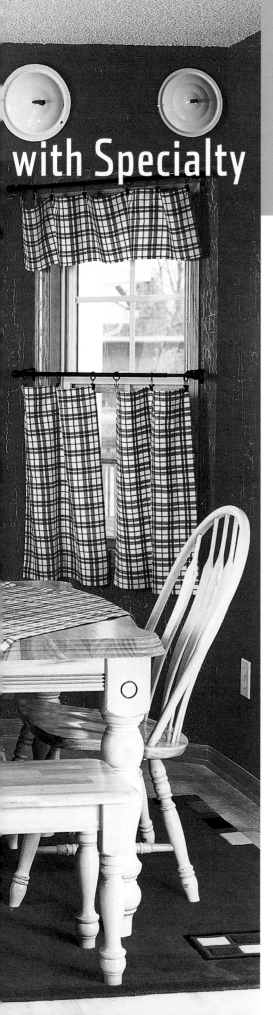

with Specialty

Tools

The TECHNIQUES FEATURED in SECTION ONE incorporate the **positive or negative application of a glaze/paint mixture**, while those covered in Section Two require **precise measuring to create exact geometric designs**. This section is filled with a **wide range of techniques**, each of which uses a special tool—for instance feathers or a rocking tool—or requires a little imagination—like calligraphy or crackling—to accomplish. The final techniques aren't actually painting techniques at all, but the way in which they **incorporate paint or emulate its appearance** makes them worthy of inclusion.

CALLIGRAPHY

HAND LETTERING CAN BE CREATED IN ANY FORM DESIRED, from whimsical flowing script to big block letters—calligraphy isn't limited to formal typefaces. Hand lettering is one of the most versatile painting techniques: Whether you paint letters freehand, use carbon copy paper to transfer the letters (as described on page 121), stencil them (see page 134), or utilize a projector (see page 124), you can create a wide range of lettering styles in whatever color of acrylic paint, paint pen, or even permanent marker you desire. If you choose to paint freehand, first use a primed sample board to try out various styles and colors before committing to your walls or other project surface. For either the carbon copy or projector methods, you can use your own handwriting or select a typeface from a computer program.

Regardless of which method you choose, if you are planning to use type as a border or would like the writing to be in a straight line, use a colored pencil to mark a line for the letters to rest on; a yardstick and level or chalk line will make this job very easy. If desired, you also can mark a line where the top of each letter will rest; this is especially helpful if you hand letter.

▲ French phrases ebb and flow throughout the walls of this bathroom. The freehand purple writing starts around the mirror, and then, for interest, some sayings are painted smaller and in a lighter color, while others flow onto the adjacent walls.

hand-lettered for a kid

◀ Hand lettering is not for walls only: Furniture pieces with flat, open spaces, like this chest of drawers in a young boy's room, are ideal places to showcase hand lettering. This charming piece also incorporates sponging on the drawer fronts and hand-painted stars. See page 70 for more information on sponging and page 122 for hand painting.

blackboard paint

MAKING A CUSTOM-SIZE BLACKBOARD is quite easy and it provides a surface that you can write on over and over again. The secret to this project is blackboard paint that comes in either a can or in a spray form. One coat covers most surfaces and dries in about four hours. To create a "blackboard" such as the one shown here, paint the wall in the desired area, paint or stain moldings that have been cut to size, and then attach to the wall to frame the painted area.

inspired dining

▲ A combination of hand lettering (using the carbon-copy paper method) and stenciled flowers makes this dining area a gardener's dream. See page 134 for more information on stenciling.

▼ Words flow freely around this casual dining space. The old Irish proverb, which is situated between white painted crown molding and wide fabric ribbon, is created with the help of a projector. The outlined letters are filled in with a paint marker.

lettering options

IF YOU ARE NOT CONFIDENT in your ability to write legibly on a vertical wall surface but love the look of calligraphy, fear not! There are numerous options for the faint-of-heart, including handmade or purchased stencils, rub-on letters, and images projected onto the wall with an overhead projector. Regardless of which method you choose, to ensure your letters are even and straight, use a level and a pencil to lightly draw horizontal guide lines on which your letters will rest and fall between (which is especially helpful if you are working on more than one line of text).

the **CALLIGRAPHY** technique

■ As described on page 118, there are numerous options for enhancing walls and other paintable surfaces with lettering, but the following carbon copy paper method is the easiest, especially if you are uneasy about writing freehand on a vertical wall surface. After tracing the letters onto the project surface, fill in the letters with acrylic paint, paint markers, or even permanent markers.

YOU WILL NEED

☐ Latex paint for base coat in desired color and finish

☐ Acrylic paint, paint markers, or permanent markers in desired colors

☐ Carbon copy paper

☐ Pencil

☐ Optional: Artist's paintbrush

☐ Optional: Computer and printer

HOW-TO steps

1. Apply the base coat to the surface; let dry.

2. Select the desired words or verse. Decide if you are going to use your own penmanship or a readymade font from a computer word processing program. If you use a computer, choose a font, auditioning different sizes, and print the words onto paper.

3. Decide where you want the letters to appear on the project surface. Place the paper with the carbon side toward the surface. Lay the type over the carbon paper and trace over the letter outlines with the pencil. Make dark marks to ensure the letters are transferred onto the project surface. **(Photo A)**

4. Lift away the carbon paper and fill in the outlined letters with the acrylic paint and artist's paintbrush, or with paint or permanent markers. **(Photo B)**

calligraphy **tools**

A variety of markers, including paint, permanent, and calligraphy, can be used for hand lettering. If you are not confident enough to letter freehand, use carbon copy paper to transfer your design onto the wall or piece of furniture as described above.

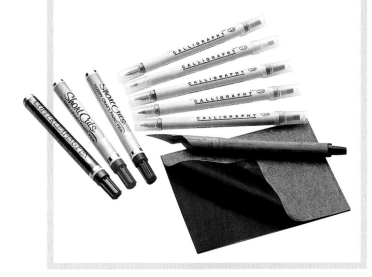

HAND-PAINTED MOTIFS

DO YOU LOVE THE LOOK OF STENCILING, but prefer a more freehand, looser appearance? If so, try hand painting motifs on your walls or other project surfaces. You can easily embellish these surfaces with polka dots, swirls, or wavy lines with acrylic paints, paint markers, or even permanent markers. If you want to create a repeated, straight-line pattern, for instance a border, measure and mark a line lightly with a pencil or snap a chalk line on which the motifs will be placed; otherwise, randomly place the motifs on the surface for a true freeform effect.

◀ Bursting with color, this bathroom is sure to lure in even the fussiest child at bath time. Aqua blue walls are the perfect backdrop for simple hand-painted polka dots, while clean white tiles in the shower showcase vivid dots of various sizes. Even the floor gets in on the fun: Random tiles get a hand-painted gingham treatment in a rainbow of colors. See page 104 for information on creating a gingham pattern. ▼

TIPS for success

▌ To hand-paint more precise circles, use inexpensive foam daubers, or spouncers. Pour paint onto a paper plate, dip the dauber into the paint, pounce onto the plate to remove excess paint, and then gently press onto the wall or other surface.

decorating with **whimsical** doodles

▲ This one-day decorating job requires only a thick black permanent marker—and a vivid imagination. Whimsical doodles are found all over this once all-white plain bedroom, from the walls to the lampshade and dresser.

personalized ceramic tiles

▲ You can embellish installed tiles with hand-painted look-alike motifs for maximum impact with minimal financial obligation. Rub-on transfers and enamel paint made specifically for ceramic or plastic tiles are used to jazz up the wall of this bathroom. To create freehand designs similar to these, use an accent liner available in black, white, or gold in a needle-nose bottle to paint outline designs to fill in with paint and details.

hand-painted motifs add color

▼ This pedestal table, typically used in more formal settings, seems to relax when a hand-painted flower in cheerful colors is added to its top.

▲ Believe it or not, the "swag" in this bathroom is hand-painted. After a master pattern is drawn, the design is traced around the room; fudging—making the last swag on a wall smaller or bigger according to how much room is left—keeps things even. The valance also uses the swag motif. It is painted directly onto canvas, then mounted on thin plywood and attached to the wall above the window with an L-bracket. Notice that the vertical stripes and delicate floral design just above the tiles are also hand-painted. For more information on painting stripes, see page 86.

hand-painted **stripes** are a **delight**

Loose, uneven hand-painted black and blue stripes in this bold child's bathroom are enhanced with playful fish and starfish on the walls and toilet seat cover.

the **HAND-PAINTED MOTIFS** technique

■ Before you begin hand painting a wall or other surface, experiment with numerous motifs on a primed sample board. This allows you to play with various types and sizes of motifs in different colors before you commit your time and effort to painting.

YOU WILL NEED

☐ Latex paint for base coat in desired color and finish

☐ Acrylic paint, paint markers, or permanent markers

☐ Optional: Artist's paintbrush

HOW-TO steps

1. Apply the base coat to the surface; let dry.

2. Use acrylic paint, paint markers, or permanent markers to create the desired motifs on the surface.

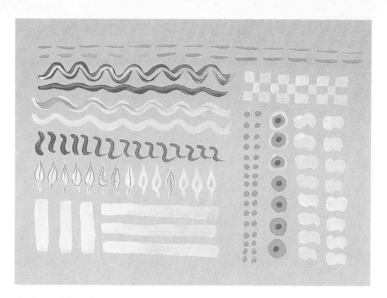

▲ A sample board is a great place on which to experiment with different color and motif options before working on a project surface.

hand-paint with ease

■ There is a wide variety of products available to make freehand painting easier: different sized brushes, acrylic paints, and even a projector that allows you to project any image—black and white or color—onto a wall surface to trace and then paint.

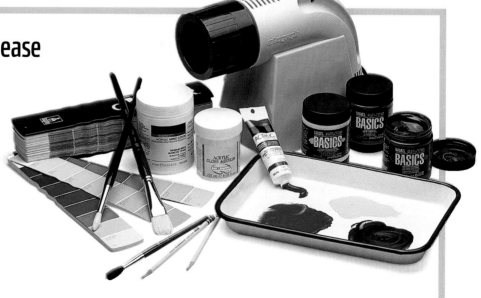

STAMPING

STAMPING CAN BE USED IN A WIDE RANGE OF HOME DECORATING STYLES, from fun and unfussy to formal, depending on the motifs chosen and the colors used. There are thousands of stamp patterns available, in sizes from small to large, and because stamps often lack crisp details, the result is a bold graphic treatment. When combined with eye-popping colors, stamps are right at home in casual spaces, such as family rooms, breakfast nooks, bathrooms, and kids' rooms; stamping in a random format works well for these applications. When a more sophisticated color palette and formal designs are used, dining rooms and living rooms can look equally as charming, especially when used in a consistent, repeated border design.

The stamps commonly used for home decorating applications are not the standard wood-mounted variety often used for paper crafts. Special foam-mounted stamps used for stamping walls and other paintable surfaces are thicker and easier to hold and use on a vertical surface than those that are wood-mounted. These stamps are often quite inexpensive and can be cleaned quickly with water and mild soap.

▲ In this teenager's room the dynamic wall treatment is based on the bright bedding. Pink-red and periwinkle hues from the bedcover are used for the stamped leaf images. The rest of the wall is filled in with a lime green paint/glaze mixture (3 parts glaze to 1 part paint) casually brushed onto a white base coat. The white background visible behind the leaves helps them stand out against the green. The stamps used here are cut from a computer mouse pad.

The outdoors is brought in with a fern-stamped floorcloth. The single- and double-fern motifs, in light and dark green, are created with thick foam stamps. See page 92 for information on creating a floorcloth.

making a stamp

■ There are thousands of stamp motifs available, but if you can't find the exact design you want, you can easily make your own from common household items.

MOUSE PAD. Draw the motif on paper; cut out. Trace the motif onto the mouse pad. (Photo A) Cut out the design with scissors or a crafts knife. (Photo B) To use the stamp, roll paint onto it with a small foam roller and apply to the project surface in the desired pattern.

A

B

COMPRESSED SPONGE. Trace or draw a design onto a sheet of flat sponge. Cut out the design with scissors and dampen the stamp with water, causing it to expand. Wring out as much water as possible before stamping.

next stop: bubble-bath junction

▲ What boy or girl wouldn't love a cheerful train chugging across the bathroom? A hand-stamped track and trains motif—inspired by an appliquéd design on the window treatment—trails around the walls and bathtub in this fun space. The top two-thirds of the walls are treated to colorwashed stripes in white and sunny yellow. See page 32 for more information on colorwashing and page 86 for creating stripes.

combining stamps

GEOMETRIC-SHAPE STAMPS can be combined to make a multitude of designs. For the train design a variety of circles, rectangles, and squares cut from craft foam are used to create the tracks and individual cars of the train.

stamp out the ordinary kitchen

▲ A funky floral design in a cool blue flows around the colorwashed walls of this cute kitchen. The curvy string of flowers breaks up the numerous square edges in the kitchen. The cabinet hardware inspired the stamped design. See page 32 for more information on colorwashing.

fun motifs on the floor

Pretty swirls stamped in light pink adorn the floor of this charming bathroom. For tips on painting vinyl flooring, see page 22.

the STAMPING technique

■ Choose foam stamps that suit the look you want to achieve; if you can't find exactly what you are looking for, make a stamp of your own design (see page 129). Don't limit yourself to one color of paint for each stamp: If you use cosmetic sponges or a small artist's paintbrush to apply paint to your stamp you can easily use various colors on appropriate parts of the stamp. Otherwise a small foam roller can be used to evenly cover a stamp with one color of paint.

YOU WILL NEED

- ☐ **Latex paint for base coat in desired color and finish**
- ☐ **Foam stamp in desired motif**
- ☐ **Acrylic paint in desired colors**
- ☐ **Cosmetic sponges, foam roller, or artist's paintbrush**
- ☐ **Paper plates**
- ☐ **Paintbrush or roller and paint tray**

HOW-TO steps

1. Apply the base coat to the surface; let dry.

2. Pour paint onto a paper plate. Using a cosmetic sponge, artist's paintbrush, or foam roller, apply an even layer of paint onto the raised design of the stamp. (Photo A)

3. Press the stamp onto the wall, using even pressure. Carefully lift the stamp from the wall.

4. Continue stamping the surface. Stamp in a repeated fashion for a border or stamp randomly for a more informal look. (Photo B)

5. Once you are done stamping, touch up any areas that didn't stamp completely with an artist's paintbrush.

A

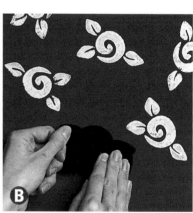

B

TIPS for success

■ Dipping the stamp directly in the paint often results in the stamp becoming too saturated, which will result in uneven, unsatisfactory results.

foam stamps

Special foam stamps—which are larger and easier to hold than smaller rubber stamps used for various paper crafts—make embellishing walls and other paintable surfaces quick and easy. Foam stamps are available in nearly every motif imaginable. If you can't find the motifs you desire for your particular project, you can easily make your own; see page 129 for more information. Small tubes of acrylic craft paint are very economical for stamping; cosmetic sponges are great paint applicators.

STENCILING

STENCILING IS A TECHNIQUE WITH LIMITLESS POSSIBILITIES: Stencils are available in nearly every motif and size imaginable. They can be combined for one-of-a-kind looks, used to create a continuous border pattern or in a random allover design, and nearly any surface—from walls and furniture to tile, fabric, and floors—can be stenciled. Further, stenciling can look very dramatic when applied over a variety of the techniques featured in this book, including ragging, sponging, and colorwashing.

There are numerous types of stencils available, from simple single-layer designs where you only require one stencil to complete the motif, to more complex multiple-layer designs where individual stencils are layered atop one another to complete the motif. Sturdy home

▲ When adding design interest is a goal, consider geometric motifs as an alternative to more complex designs. Such patterns detail plain spaces without taking charge of the decor, especially when created in a flowing, repeated pattern. Echoing the lines of the cast-iron railing, the stylized pattern details the risers in this stairway. The repetition of black throughout lends a sophisticated note to the space.

decorating stencils made of Mylar or plastic can be found in thousands of designs suitable for all your decorating needs, but they can also be made if you can't find the exact design you want (see page 137 for information). Stencil plastic is available where you purchase ready-made stencils, while larger stencil board is often available at crafts stores. Either of these materials will be very durable and long-lasting. Mylar can be found by the yard at art supply stores, making it ideal for large stencils, but this material tends to tear easily (although it can be mended with tape).

One of the keys to successful stenciling is using the right supplies: adhesives, brushes, and paints. First, in order to keep stencils in place as you are working on a vertical or horizontal surface and to prevent paint from seeping beneath the stencil (often referred to as "bleeding"), use a low-tack, repositionable tape or spray adhesive. These products are readily available at crafts and art supply stores. Next you will need to invest in quality stenciling brushes. These stiff-bristle brushes come in a wide variety of sizes to accommodate stencils with varying amounts of details. If you plan to stencil multiple colors for one project, it is wise to have one brush for each color. Finally, paints are what truly bring a stenciled design to life. You can use a wide variety of paints and colorings for stenciling, including acrylic paints, stencil creams, and stencil crayons. Acrylic paints dry quickly, making color layering easy; further, acrylic paints are easy to clean from the stencil surface with water and mild soap. Stencil creams are of a soft consistency and are easy to work with. Stencil crayons are very similar in nature to creams, but instead of picking up paint directly from a jar, you must scribble the crayon onto a paper plate and then pick up the color with a brush.

stenciling **tools**

Stencils in nearly every size and motif imaginable are readily available for all of your home decorating needs. Specially formulated stencil crayons, creams, and even acrylic paints can be used with stencils.

stenciled motifs unify a space

▲ Allover stenciled designs in soft colors, such as the basket-weave on these once-drab closet doors, warm a room without dominating. The pattern repeats in a pair of accent pillows to unify the scheme. Touches of red in this room introduce splashes of warm color, while light wood and wicker accessories add to the natural style. See page 144 for information on stenciling fabric.

cleaning and storing stencils

To ensure your stencils and supplies last a lifetime, follow these cleaning and storage tips:

■ Clean stencils immediately after use with water, mild soap, and a sponge. Dry with a towel. Store stencils flat to prevent bending and bowing.

■ Clean brushes immediately after use with warm water or a specially formulated brush cleaner. Allow to dry naturally and store in a cup or other container with the bristles up.

making stencils

■ Stencils come in nearly every design imaginable, but you can easily make your own from stencil plastic or another stencil material for a personalized look. When choosing a motif, make sure the design elements are not too large or shaped in a way that makes stenciling difficult. Ensure that the designs you select are copyright free.

▲ Use these readily available tools and materials to make your own stencils.

HOW-TO steps

1. Draw or trace the desired motif onto paper. When you are satisfied with the design, transfer it to the stencil material. If you use translucent stencil plastic, place the pattern underneath the plastic and trace with a fine-tip marker. If the plastic isn't large enough, tape two pieces together. If you use opaque poster board, transfer the pattern onto the board with carbon copy paper.

2. If the stencil will be used for a repeated design, for instance a border, create a registration mark that will help you line up the design. In the example shown, a portion of the leaf motif is drawn on the edge of the left-hand side so it can be lined up with the motif to be stenciled once the stencil is moved.

3. Using a self-healing cutting mat, cut out the stenciled designs with a crafts knife. (**Photo A**) Be sure to have extra blades on hand and switch to sharp blades as often as necessary to ensure crisp cuts. Note that some knives, like that shown, have comfort grips, which reduce hand and finger fatigue while you are cutting.

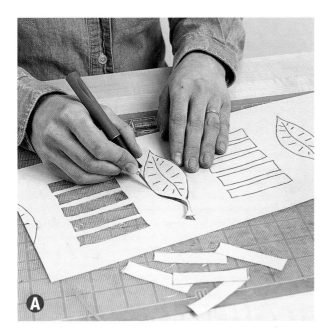

Ⓐ

rub a dub dub **ducks**

▲ The lighthearted style of this bathroom is achieved through a variety of techniques, the most charming of which are stenciled rubber ducks. The bright yellow ducks waddling around the room and over the mirror and window stand out from the blue colorwashed background. The hand-painted border and vertical stripes complete the look. See page 32 for more information on colorwashing, page 122 for hand painting, and page 86 for creating stripes.

◀ If stenciling is too time-consuming for you, but you love the look of the technique, try one of the many borders currently available that are easy to apply to a wall and have the look of stenciling.

▶ Rich gold walls are the perfect backdrop for lively stenciled flowers in this cheerful nursery. The ceiling is given a chance to shine with a freeflowing wavy vine and stenciled flower motif border, while the inner portion is treated with a swirly green paint and glaze mixture (3 parts glaze to 1 part paint). The hand-painted floor design grounds the room. Brightly colored bedding, simple felt valances, and playful flower drawer pulls complete the look. See page 32 for more information on colorwashing and page 122 for hand-painting tips.

cocktail **dreams**

▲ Stenciled martini glasses provide an appropriate backdrop for a vintage bar, barstools, a retro pendant light, and bamboo shades. The classic martini glass, with a pimento-stuffed olive, tilts as part of its casual charm.

project: stenciled relief pattern

■ Transforming unfinished furniture into finished pieces that appear as though they have delicate carving is achieved with a plasterlike product and a thick (¼-inch or more) stencil. If you have difficulties finding a thick stencil, adhere two or three of the same design together.

YOU WILL NEED

- ☐ Latex paint for base coat in neutral color
- ☐ Stencil in desired motif
- ☐ Stencil adhesive spray or low-tack tape
- ☐ Putty knife
- ☐ Plaster
- ☐ Paintbrush and paint tray
- ☐ Stiff-bristle paintbrush
- ☐ Amber glaze
- ☐ Lint-free cloth

HOW-TO steps

1. Set the stencil on the furniture piece in the desired location. Using a putty knife, fill in the stencil with the plaster. (Photo A) Immediately remove the stencil and allow the plaster to dry. Note that if you make a mistake, you can wipe the plaster away while it is still wet, or sand it away after it's dry and start again.

2. Paint the entire piece of furniture with the neutral base coat; let dry.

3. To achieve the subtly aged look of the bookcases shown here, use a stiff-bristle brush to apply a small amount of amber glaze over the entire piece, allowing it to sink into the crevices. (Photo B) Then go back with a dry, clean cloth and wipe the glaze off the top of the relief pattern. The dark color adds shadow and definition to the pattern.

Oversize leaves—inspired by the area rug in this sunroom—draw the eye upward. The leaves bend and flow around the ceiling and top portion of the wall.

borders and corners

When stenciling a border—or even a random pattern that wraps from a wall to the ceiling, for example—corners and ending perfectly are issues that you must deal with.

■ For corners, try bending your stencil into the corner to get the image exactly where it is supposed to be. If this doesn't work, you can measure the "run" (the length) of the stencil, skip the corner, leaving the exact size of one run blank, then stencil the corner last. This way, the rest of your room is already complete, and you can cut the stencil to fit the remaining space.

■ What do you do when you are at the end of your stenciled border, and you only have room for two-thirds of the stencil run? You "fudge it." Often you do not have to complete the entire run to make the stenciled design look good. Consider several options: First complete the partial run so that it visually flows with the rest of the border design. Second if you anticipate you will come up short as you near the end of your project, consider adjusting the spaces between the last few runs. Finally cut a new custom stencil to complete the project.

motifs by the **door**

▲ Stenciled with white latex paint, a beautiful flowing rose motif embellishes the windows surrounding this entryway door. The paint can be scraped off with a razor blade when you want a change.

▼ Exterior view

stenciling on fabric

■ It's as easy to apply stenciled designs to fabric as to walls. First wash the fabric to be embellished. Do not use detergent or fabric softener; they may affect the way in which the paint adheres to the fabric. Dry the fabric; iron. Mix the desired acrylic paint with a textile medium in the ratio provided on the bottle's instructions. Lay the fabric taut on a plastic-covered surface; secure with tape.

If you stencil on a double-thickness fabric, such as a pillowcase, put a piece of cardboard or posterboard cut to size between the layers prior to stenciling to avoid bleeding paint. Position the stencil as desired on the fabric. Apply the textile medium/paint mixture with a stenciling brush in a dabbing motion, as you would for any other surface. Set the fabric as directed for permanency and washability.

▲ Inspired by the embroidered window treatment, the walls, bedding, and window seat cushion are embellished with stenciled designs.

the STENCILING technique

■ Stenciling can be used successfully in rooms of every style; if you can't find the exact motif you are looking for, make your own stencil (see page 137 for information). Basic stenciling in one color—using a single layer stencil—is by far the easiest method; stenciling becomes more difficult as you incorporate additional colors and use multi-layer stencils. If you make a mistake, immediately use a clean cotton cloth with a little water to wipe the paint away. Allow the area to dry and restencil.

YOU WILL NEED

- [ ] **Latex paint for base coat in desired color and finish**
- [ ] **Stencil in desired motif**
- [ ] **Acrylic paint, stencil crayons, or stencil cream in desired colors**
- [ ] **Stencil adhesive spray or low-tack tape**
- [ ] **Stenciling brush, one for each color**
- [ ] **Paper plate**
- [ ] **Paintbrush or roller and paint tray**
- [ ] **Optional: Chalk line, yardstick, level**
- [ ] **Optional: Acrylic polyurethane**

HOW-TO steps

1. Apply the base coat to the surface; let dry.

2. If you are stenciling in a repeated motif (i.e., a border), use a chalk line or yardstick and level to mark where the edge of the stencil should be placed.

3. Spray adhesive on the back of the stencil and press it against the wall in the desired position.

4. Pour acrylic paint onto a paper plate. If using stencil crayons, scribble some color onto a paper plate. If using stencil cream, you can dip the brush directly into the pot. Dampen the brush slightly with water and shake out any excess. Dip the brush into the paint and dab off any excess. Don't overload paint onto the brush; this will encourage paint to seep under the stencil.

5. Using a circular or dabbing motion, apply paint to the stencil's open portions; let dry slightly. (Photo A)

6. Remove the stencil and place it in the next desired location on the wall, using the registration marks, if applicable, as a guide. If paint has seeped to the back of the stencil, wipe it away before repositioning it to avoid smudges.

7. Repeat Step 6 until you have achieved the desired look. Let the paint dry completely.

8. If desired, apply acrylic polyurethane to the stenciled areas if they receive heavy use or may require cleaning and/or scrubbing.

Ⓐ

MARBLING

THERE ARE LITERALLY THOUSANDS OF COLORS, STYLES, AND TYPES OF MARBLE. This cool, smooth stone adds opulence to a home—but its expense does not allow many to enjoy it, especially in large doses. If you love the look of marble, but are weary of spending a small fortune, paint it: While the technique described on page 149 is time-consuming, it can add a rich look and feel to any paintable surface, from walls to fireplace mantels, floors, and tabletops.

Before you begin, examine different types of marbles to select which you would like to duplicate in paint. Look at the subtle color shifts in the background and the thickness, colors, and frequency of the veins. If you plan to paint a large area, map out your design: To emulate real marble, paint the surface in tilelike panels. If a large area is daunting, try the technique in smaller areas, perhaps enclosed in molding.

The basic marble technique incorporates numerous steps and tools. First, to create the multi-color mottled background, use the leather technique, as described on page 56: Paint the desired base coat, allow to dry, paint with the top coat paint, then press and peel away plastic wrap. Finally, paint the veins with a feather and soften and blend with a veining brush.

◀ An allover marble treatment is a sophisticated backdrop for this traditional setting. The main portions of the walls are covered with a rich brown pattern, while the top portion between the molding and the ceiling features pale creams and grays. Gold-accented furnishings and accessories throughout the room play off the walls, while a distressed fireplace mantel is right at home. See page 154 for information on distressing.

marbling **the mantel**

▲ A contemporary take on marble makes a playful addition to this mantel. Light beige covers the entire mantel, while the trim is accented with the same red paint that is found on the surrounding wall. Marble in white, black, and red graces the recessed areas. See page 148 for information on painting wood.

is it real **marble**?

▲ Painted marble in shades of cream and gold mimic the real marble that graces a shelf ledges (not shown) in this traditional dining room. The marble is used sparingly as an accent: Small portions of the wall are given the treatment, then they are surrounded by painted moldings cut to size as "frames." Above the chair rail, tailored colorwashed stripes lend a sophisticated air. See page 32 for more information on colorwashing and page 86 for creating stripes.

preparing wood for painting

If you plan to apply a marble finish to a piece of wood furniture, a fireplace mantel, or molding, you must first prime it, let the primer dry, then lightly sand it. Then apply the base coat to the primed and sanded surface before proceeding with the instructions on page 149.

the **MARBLING** technique

■ Marbling can be a difficult technique to master, but the results are definitely worth the effort, especially if you love the rich look of the real thing but it doesn't fit into your budget. Remember to look at examples of real marble before beginning a project to get a sense of how the veins mingle and meander on the background. You will notice that many types of real marble have softly blended backgrounds. In the following instructions, you will use the basic leather technique (as described on page 59) to blend colors for a similar look.

YOU WILL NEED

- ☐ Satin or semi-gloss latex paint for base coat in desired color
- ☐ Satin or semi-gloss latex paint for top coat in desired color
- ☐ Acrylic paints in desired colors
- ☐ Painter's tape
- ☐ Plastic wrap
- ☐ Paintbrush and softening brush
- ☐ Feather
- ☐ Lint-free cloth

HOW-TO steps

1. Apply the base coat to the project surface; let dry.

2. Divide the wall into a sequence of panels, each approximately 4 feet square. Mask off alternating sections using painter's tape.

3. Apply the top coat to one section of the wall with a damp, wadded lint-free cloth. (Photo A)

4. While the top coat is wet, press a piece of plastic onto the wall, smoothing it with your hand or a brush. Carefully peel the plastic off the wall. (Photo B) If the lines are too dramatic, use the softening brush to blend the background for a more natural, mottled finish. Let the paint dry. (Photo C)

5. Use the edge and tip of the feather to apply thin lines of acrylic paint to the painted section. Drag the feather over the surface in diagonal lines of different lengths, using varying amounts of pressure and twisting the feather for more natural-looking lines. (Photo D)

6. While the veins are still wet, blend them with the softening brush. (Photo E) Remove the tape; let the paint dry.

7. Continue the marbling process for every masked-off (alternating) section, as described in Steps 3 through 6.

8. Mask off each unpainted section. Apply the top coat paint and repeat the entire process as described in Steps 3 through 7 until the entire wall is complete.

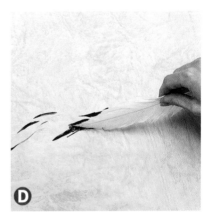

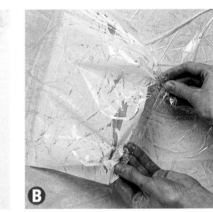

TIPS for success

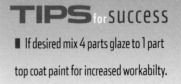

■ If desired mix 4 parts glaze to 1 part top coat paint for increased workabilty.

WOOD GRAINING

ONE OF THE MOST DRAMATIC AND IMPRESSIVE TECHNIQUES, wood graining can easily be accomplished with the use of a specialty wood-graining tool. This tool, which is widely available at crafts stores and home improvement centers, is simply dragged and rocked through a top coat of paint to reveal some of the base coat color. The resulting "grain" looks like silk moiré fabric. Because it may be difficult to keep the tool steady as you drag it down a wall or across a flat, horizontal surface, you may find it easier to work within smaller areas, such as below a chair rail or within a section of molding.

▲ The elegant, European look of moiré lends pattern to this casual space, but doesn't overwhelm because it is used only on the bottom portion of the wall. Very pale blue and medium blue are used under the chair rail. For a more rustic , wood-paneled effect, tan and walnut colors may be used.

project: wood-grained metal

It is easy to give a plain metal file cabinet the look of wood: All you need are a wood-graining tool and heavy-bodied wood stain. While anyone can tackle this project, it is recommended that you practice using the wood-graining tool on a primed sample board to get the feel of it.

YOU WILL NEED

- ☐ Satin or semi-gloss latex paint for base coat in neutral color
- ☐ Mineral spirits
- ☐ Wood stain
- ☐ Polyurethane
- ☐ Lint-free cloths
- ☐ Wood-graining tool
- ☐ Foam brush
- ☐ Paintbrush and paint tray
- ☐ Metal file cabinet
- ☐ Rubber gloves

HOW-TO steps

1. Apply the base coat to the cabinet and drawer fronts; let dry. Dampen a cloth with mineral spirits; wipe the mineral spirits onto the cabinet and drawer fronts.

2. Use the lint-free cloth to wipe a thin, uniform coat of wood stain on one drawer front.

3. While wearing rubber gloves, create a horizontal grain on the drawer, following the instructions on page 153. If you make a mistake, just wipe on more stain and try again. Clean the tool occasionally so it doesn't clog. Continue creating the wood-grain pattern on the drawer, using the previous grainline as a guide. (Photo A)

4. Repeat Steps 2 and 3 on the other drawer and then the top and sides of the cabinet. Create a horizontal pattern on the drawers and cabinet top, but use a vertical grain on the cabinet sides. When all sections have been completed, let the file cabinet dry for 24 to 48 hours.

5. Use the foam brush or lint-free cloth to wipe on a thin, uniform coat of stain. Apply the stain in the direction of the grain pattern. (Photo B) Use a dry paintbrush to gently feather streaks and lap marks. Let dry 24 to 48 hours.

6. Brush on a coat of polyurethane.

silk look-alike

The allover green moiré pattern on this sitting room wall resembles an expensive silk wallcovering.

the **WOOD-GRAINING** technique

■ Like many of the "negative" techniques featured in Section One, the wood-graining technique requires a steady hand: You must quickly and evenly move a tool down or across the still-wet surface to create visual texture and reveal some of the base coat color. As with many of the techniques in this book, it pays to spend time practicing with the tool—and experimenting with varying top and base coat color combinations—on a primed sample board before committing time and energy to a wall or other project surface.

YOU WILL NEED

- ☐ Satin or semi-gloss latex paint for base coat in desired color
- ☐ Satin or semi-gloss latex paint for top coat in desired color
- ☐ Wood-graining tool
- ☐ Lint-free cloth
- ☐ Paintbrush or roller and paint tray
- ☐ Optional: Glaze, bucket, and mixing tool

HOW-TO steps

1. Apply the base coat to the surface; let dry.

2. Brush or roll the top coat paint onto an approximate 2- to 3-foot vertical section of the wall.

3. Starting at the top of the just-painted section, pull the wood-graining tool down the wall, exerting pressure with your index finger and rocking the tool from top to bottom in one continuous motion. The tool will form a varied series of long, concentric "ovals." Use the previously grained strip as a guide (lining up edge of tool with section just painted) and be sure to stagger the pattern so that it does not appear too uniform. (**Photo A**) Wipe the excess paint from the tool after each pass.

4. Repeat the painting and wood-graining process, working in 2- to 3-foot vertical sections, until the entire wall is complete.

Ⓐ

TIPS for success

■ For longer workability of the top coat, mix the paint with glaze in a 4 parts glaze to 1 part paint ratio.

WOOD-GRAINING TOOL

■ An inexpensive **wood-graining tool** is used to create **elongated oval shapes** on a wall or other **paintable surface** for this technique.

DISTRESSING

IF YOU LOVE ALL THINGS OLD, AGED, AND GENERALLY "BEAT UP," but you are fearful of lead paints or don't want to invest in antique pieces, you can give new furniture a worn look with the distressing technique. While this technique is most commonly associated with a country decorating style, it can look charming in rooms of nearly any style if appropriate colors are chosen.

Distressing, which is done on wood surfaces, including beaded board, furniture, cabinets, floors, and even staircases, is time-consuming—the process involves painting, sanding, and staining—but the results are particularly pleasing. Natural distressing occurs because of changes in humidity, use, and exposure to the elements: Layers of paint will wear away, revealing older paint and natural wood beneath. When a piece is distressed using the steps outlined on page 159, you will cause layers of paint to be removed by sanding. If you examine antique pieces where natural distressing has occurred, you will see that most of the chipped or loose paint appears in areas that would have received the most wear, for instance raised surfaces or around handles. Generally, recessed areas don't show excessive amounts of wear. Keep this in mind as you distress your project surfaces.

Similar to the crackling technique, described on page 160, distressing lends itself to contrasting colors. When you select paints, keep in mind that the top coat paint will be most visible and only small portions of the base coat will be exposed.

choosing furniture to distress

■ If the look of distressed furnishings appeals to you but you don't want to experiment with Grandma's blanket chest, look for paintable furniture that has decorating potential at flea markets, secondhand stores, and antique shops; often the investment is minimal, and you may be surprised by the quality and selection these outlets offer. Examine pieces for sturdiness and condition, understanding that you may need to make minor repairs. Determine whether the surfaces are paintable, whether obvious damage can be repaired, and whether the repairs warrant the cost and work involved.

■ Another option to consider is inexpensive unfinished wood furnishings.

distressed by hand

▲ Distressing produces a cupboard that reflects a refined rustic setting. Reproduction pulls furnish an authentic touch, while colorwashed walls in rich greens and yellows provide textural contrast for the distinctive piece. See page 32 for information on colorwashing.

distressed diamonds on the rise

▲ Unconventional spaces are the perfect places to showcase a distressed finish. These stair risers, embellished with hand-painted diamonds, are distressed for a worn, aged appearance. To complement the look, the walls are colorwashed. See page 32 for information on colorwashing and page 106 for creating diamonds.

two-hued distressing

▲ ► Bright, dramatic red and soft, sunny butter yellow lend a fresh feel to these kitchen cabinets. Toile wallpaper and other accessories—in red and white—pull the look together.

beyond basic **beaded board**

▲ ▶ Beaded-board wainscoting can simply be painted with a solid color of paint, but distressing gives it a charming weathered look, as in this small powder room.

the DISTRESSING technique

■ When selecting colors for this technique, remember that the base coat color will only peek through the top coat where the top coat is sanded away. Also keep in mind that most of the sanding should be where natural wear—for instance around handles and on raised portions of the project surface—would occur.

YOU WILL NEED

☐ **Latex primer**

☐ **Latex paint for base coat in desired color and finish**

☐ **Latex paint for top coat in desired color and finish**

☐ **Medium-grit sandpaper**

☐ **Tack cloth**

☐ **Lint-free cloths**

☐ **Paintbrushes and paint tray**

☐ **Water-base stain, in desired finish**

☐ **Optional: Wax or water-base polyurethane**

HOW-TO steps

1. Prime the surface to be distressed; let dry.

2. Lightly sand the entire surface. Wipe away any dust with a tack cloth.

3. Apply the base coat to the surface; let dry.

4. If desired apply wax to the surface.

5. Apply the top coat paint to the surface; let dry.

6. Sand the raised portions of the surface, rubbing away paint in the natural wear areas. (Photo A) Wipe away any dust with a tack cloth.

7. Randomly brush stain onto one area of the project surface. Quickly wipe away some of the stain with a lint-free cloth, allowing it to sink into any recessed areas. (Photo B) Continue applying and removing stain until the entire surface has been covered.

8. If desired rub the entire painted surface with wax or apply polyurethane for protection.

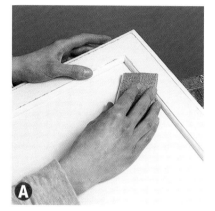
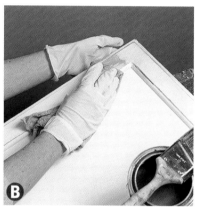

CRACKLING

ONE OF THE MOST EXCITING—AND SOMETIMES MOST UNPREDICTABLE—paint techniques featured in this book is crackling. While true crackling and crazing on antique wood furnishings and accessories is caused by changes in humidity and weather, the crackling technique is achieved when a specially formulated crackle medium is applied over a base coat, and then a top coat in a contrasting color is painted over the cured medium. The crackle medium will cause the top coat paint to stretch and split, exposing some of the base coat. This aging treatment is commonly used on furnishings, but walls are also a great place to showcase the technique.

Perhaps one of the most interesting aspects of this technique is its versatility. By altering the amount of crackle medium applied to the surface, the type of tool used to apply the top coat, and the pressure used to apply it, you can create wildly different looks. Generally, using a roller with heavy pressure will result in fine, tiny spider-veinlike cracks, whereas brushing with light pressure will create wide, thick cracks. You can also use a sea sponge to apply the top coat; rather than vertical or horizontal cracks, random splits will occur on the project surface

◀ ▲ Irregular weblike cracks lend charm to this casual dining area. Builder white walls serve as the base coat, and a bright, bold red is used for the top coat. The simple window treatments and partially whitewashed furnishings complement the crackle finish. See page 164 for more information on whitewashing.

(see page 207 for an example).

When you plan a crackle project, think about contrast: Remember that the top coat will be most visible and that the base coat will show through in the split areas. Choose colors that have enough contrast to showcase the technique; however, too much contrast can look awkward. Let the styles and colors of the furnishings and other accessories in the room be your guide. And always use a sample board to test out your chosen color combination before committing it to your wall or project surface.

Unfinished furniture painted with bold red, blue, and yellow makes a big splash—with little financial investment. The tabletop and bench tops are given a crackle treatment for added interest. To paint unfinished furniture for the outdoors, use exterior primer and paint, and coat the surfaces with a suitable weatherproof sealer after the paint dries. You can use exterior paints with crafts store crackle medium as long as a water-base variety is chosen.

crackling and stenciling

WITH AN OLD-WORLD CRACKLE FINISH and wispy poppies that appear to be gently floating down to rest on the bed, this serene scene invites slumber. Contrasting colors used on the wall—poppy red as a base coat and lime green as a top coat—define the bed and stenciled area. The randomly scattered flowers above the bed and on the ceiling give the room additional dimension and create a custom look that would be difficult to achieve with wallpaper. For more information on stenciling, see page 134.

the CRACKLING technique

■ The crackling technique is truly unpredictable, which may seem daunting to the faint of heart, but if you like surprises, this technique is a great one to try. Remember to use a primed sample board to practice the technique with various application tools and amounts of pressure, as well as color combinations, to find the look that will best suit your project.

YOU WILL NEED

☐ Flat or eggshell latex paint for base coat in desired color

☐ Flat or eggshell latex paint for top coat in desired color

☐ Crackle medium

☐ Paintbrushes or rollers and paint tray

☐ Optional: Sea sponge

☐ Optional: Water-base polyurethane

HOW-TO steps

1. Apply the base coat to the surface; let dry.

2. Following the manufacturer's directions, apply the crackle medium to the project surface. Allow the medium to cure the recommended length of time.

3. Apply the top coat paint with a paintbrush, roller, or sea sponge. (**Photo A**) Varying the application pressure will result in different looks. Do not overlap the top coat paint application once crackling has begun. Allow the paint to dry.

4. If desired apply an even coat of water-base polyurethane to the project surface for protection.

CRACKLING DOs and DON'Ts

■ **DO** use a primed sample board to experiment with different thicknesses of crackle medium and top coat application tools and pressures.

■ **DO** read the crackle medium manufacturer's directions carefully before beginning your project; product curing time and application methods will vary by manufacturer. Note that some prepackaged crackle kits require two separate products and steps while others involve only one.

■ **DO** brush or roll all top coat paint in one direction (vertical or horizontal) on the project surface to keep the cracks running in one direction. Keep this in mind when you cut in a wall or ceiling.

■ **DO** use a flat or eggshell paint for both the base coat and top coat. Other paint finishes may not work with your chosen crackle medium.

■ **DO** seal the completed project with a coat of water-base polyurethane if the project surface will receive heavy use or exposure to the elements.

■ **DO** enlist a partner if you are crackling a large area; you need to cover the entire area with the top coat within the time specified by the crackle medium's manufacturer. Ensure you both use the same top-coat application tools and methods for consistent results.

■ **DON'T** repaint sections that have already been painted with the top coat. This will cause the paint to lift away and smear, disturbing the crackle finish.

WHITEWASHING

WHITEWASHING, ALSO KNOWN AS PICKLING OR LIMING, is a great way to add charm to any unfinished wood surface, including floors, furniture, and beaded board. For this technique white paint diluted with water is unevenly applied to the project surface, allowing some of the natural wood grain to be exposed. While this technique lends itself to country and cottage decorating styles, it can look equally as appealing in other casual settings where pastel colors are featured.

▲ This family room is anchored by a diamond-pattern floor; the fresh treatment helps the room feel cool and breezy in the summer yet cozy in the winter. After the floor is sanded, a diamond pattern is taped off. Alternating diamonds are whitewashed, and small pewter-color squares are painted in the corners. The entire floor is finished with two coats of paste wax to protect the surface from everyday use. See page 106 for more information on creating diamonds.

sweet whitewashed dreams

▲ Tall panels of whitewashed beaded board are right at home in this young girl's room. Pretty pink accessories and whimsical hand-painted bugs on the headboard are just the right complements to the paneled wallcovering. The panels are toppd with a simple shelf with a hand-painted design. See page 122 for more information on hand painting. ▶

whitewashing the door

▲ Give any door country charm with the whitewashing technique. This door is surrounded by a pretty stenciled floral design within a hand-painted wavy border. See page 134 for more information on stenciling and page 122 for hand painting.

the WHITEWASHING technique

■ You can use the whitewashing technique on any unfinished wood surface; just make sure the surface is properly sanded and wiped clean prior to painting so that the diluted paint will adhere well. Removing some of the paint to reveal the natural wood grain adds to the charm of the finished project.

YOU WILL NEED

- ☐ Latex paint in white and any desired finish
- ☐ Bucket and mixing tool
- ☐ Paintbrush and paint tray
- ☐ Sandpaper and tack cloth
- ☐ Optional: Lint-free cloth

HOW-TO steps

1. Lightly sand the entire project surface. Wipe the surface with a tack cloth to remove all dust particles.

2. Mix 2 parts white paint to 1 part water.

3. Apply the diluted paint mixture to the surface, working quickly. Continue applying the paint/water mixture to the surface until the entire surface is covered; let dry. (Photo A)

4. Optional: Immediately after painting (and before the paint has dried) use a clean lint-free cloth to wipe the surface to remove some of the paint, revealing more of the wood grain.

DOUBLE-BRUSH and DOUBLE-ROLL

DO YOU LOVE THE LOOK OF SUBTLY BLENDED COLORS, but you don't want to commit the time and energy into painting one color and then repainting portions of the wall with another? Special dual rollers and brushes are available to tackle this painting dilemma: They allow you to paint two colors at once that can be blended to the desired finish. The rollers—which are available with both smooth and sculpted covers—and brushes come with a paint tray that is divided into two sections to make loading and reloading the paint quick and easy.

While this technique is actually quite simple, choosing the right color combination can be problematic. It is recommended that you select the two paint colors from one paint card rather than two wildly different colors that can produce an unsatisfactory result. If you desire a subtle finish, choose colors with little contrast (those that are close to each other on a paint card), but bolder effects can be achieved when there is more contrast between the colors. To avoid regrets, try your chosen colors on a primed sample board.

Pretty shades of calm green and neutral cream give this comfortable bedroom just the right amount of blended color and visual texture. A white horizontal stripe divides the lower third of the wall in a lighter green finish from the darker green portion above.

double-rolling in cool blues

▲ The marbled, plaster-like effect of the walls in this casual contemporary dining room is achieved with pale and medium blues. The paint is applied with shaped foam roller covers.

CHOOSING COLORS

▌ Before committing to either a double-brush or double-roll finish, experiment with different degrees of contrast between the two colors on a primed sample board. The more widely the two shades vary, the more dramatic the effect will be.

▌ You can achieve a wide array of looks with either technique: Two yellows resemble sun-dappled walls, while two blues make a watery, cool statement.

blended grids

Softly mingled colors within 20-inch squares in a grid design provide a serene backdrop in this living room. Keeping the colors pale and just two shades apart from each other on the paint color card creates a subtle pattern you can use throughout a room. See page 94 for more information on creating grids.

the DOUBLE-BRUSH and DOUBLE-ROLL techniques

■ While there is nothing inherently difficult about this technique, selecting appropriate colors can pose a challenge: Too much contrast may give unsatisfactory results, while colors that are too similar may blend too much—defeating the goal of the technique. To avoid problems on your project surface, try out different color combinations on a primed sample board. If you desire three colors, select a complementary base coat color and allow some to be exposed from beneath the double-rolled or double-brushed colors.

YOU WILL NEED

- ☐ Optional: Latex paint for base coat in desired color and finish
- ☐ Latex paint for top coat in desired colors and finishes
- ☐ Double brush or double roller with divided tray
- ☐ Optional: Paintbrush or roller and paint tray
- ☐ Optional: Small paintbrush

HOW-TO steps

1. If desired, apply a base coat to the surface; let dry.

2. Pour the two paint colors in the divided paint tray. Dip the rollers or brushes into the paint.

3. Roll or brush the paint onto the wall, blending the colors. (**Photo A**) When needed reload the rollers or brushes with paint. If desired leave some of the base coat exposed.

4. Continue painting until all walls are covered. If needed use a small paintbrush to brush both paint colors into corners; blend. If using a double-roller, note that you may also use a smaller foam edging piece that often comes with a double-roller kit for this process.

Ⓐ

DOUBLE**ROLLER**

■ This **double roller** has **sculpted covers**. The tray is divided into two sections, one for each color of paint. Double-roller kits often come with a small edge piece to fill in corners and edges.

RECESSED DETAILS

EMBOSSED WALLCOVERINGS THAT SIMULATE TEXTURED FABRICS, SUCH AS RAW SILK AND FLECKED LINEN, have become popular in recent years. The textures add warmth to a room—and have the added benefit of hiding flaws in your walls. While these white wallcoverings can be painted with a solid color of paint and left "as is," using a squeegee to reveal the high spots, which leaves paint in the recessed areas, lends more character.

For this technique, you first paint the wallpaper a solid color and then apply a glaze/paint mixture to the surface that will in part be removed with the squeegee. This negative technique is similar to those featured in Section One, including sponging off, ragging off, and strié, where some of the top coat color is removed to reveal a portion of the base coat. Here more visual depth is achieved because the raised details of the paper will stand out against the darker recessed areas.

▲ Embossed wallpapers are readily available at specialty paint stores and home improvement centers. There are multiple motifs available to suit nearly every decorating style.

▲ Embossed wallcoverings come in a wide variety of patterns, including everything from old-fashioned floral designs to contemporary geometrics, as shown in this dining room. The paints used—steel gray as the base coat and brown as the top coat—complement the stylish dining set and modern accessories.

project: color-rubbed **medallion**

■ Surfaces other than embossed wallcoverings can also be used for the recessed detail technique. Color rubbing—when a dark top coat of paint is brushed over a lighter base coat then wiped away, leaving the dark paint in the crevices while the wiped surfaces are highlighted—adds character to this ceiling medallion, but the technique can be used on any similar architectural element.

YOU WILL NEED

- ☐ Latex paint, light color for base coat and color two or more shades darker for top coat in desired finish
- ☐ Bucket and mixing tool
- ☐ Stenciling brush
- ☐ Angled soft-bristle brush
- ☐ Soft lint-free brush
- ☐ Japan drier or other paint extender

HOW-TO steps

1. Paint the medallion with the base coat; let dry. (Photo A)

2. Dilute the darker paint with 1 part water to 4 parts paint. Force the diluted paint into the crevices of the medallion by pressing vigorously up and down over the surface with a paint-loaded stenciling brush. Work quickly in small sections; the paint does not need to be even at this point. Be sure to work the paint into all nooks and crannies, but don't allow it to puddle.

3. Again working quickly brush out the top coat paint with the angled brush so that it is relatively

even. If the paint is too dry to brush out, let it dry completely, then apply another coat of the base color and start again. **Note: If desired, use a medium, such as Japan drier, to extend the working time of the paint.**

4. Wipe the wet paint from the raised surfaces of the medallion, exposing some of the base coat. The darker color should remain in the recessed areas. The wiped areas will also show traces of the top coat, adding depth and color variation to the medallion. (Photo B)

A

B

elegantly **embossed**

▲ A sweet old-fashioned look is achieved in this breakfast nook with a delicately embossed wallcovering covered in a peach glaze. To make sure the highly patterned wallcovering doesn't overwhelm the space, it is used below shelf molding that showcases colorful vintage pottery and dishware.

embossed for the outdoors

A rustic birdhouse looks right at home perched atop a column with an aged wallpaper top. The wallpaper is cut to size and glued to the column. White satin-finish spray paint is then applied, and a mixture of walnut stain and glaze is wiped on to enhance the detailing and embossing.

the RECESSED DETAILS technique

■ White embossed wallpapers are available in many motifs, from stripes and checks to circles and floral designs, to suit a wide range of decorating tastes and styles. Select a wallcovering—and paint colors— that best reflect the look you desire.

To ensure satisfactory results, adhere a section of your chosen wallpaper to a sample board. This will allow you to experiment with various color combinations and different sized squeegees.

YOU WILL NEED

- ☐ **Semi-gloss latex paint for base coat in desired color**
- ☐ **Semi-gloss latex paint for top coat in desired color**
- ☐ **Glaze**
- ☐ **Embossed wallpaper**
- ☐ **Wallpaper supplies**
- ☐ **Bucket and mixing tool**
- ☐ **Paintbrush**
- ☐ **Squeegee**
- ☐ **Drop cloths**
- ☐ **Lint-free cloth**

HOW-TO steps

1. Following the manufacturer's instructions apply the wallpaper to the wall or other project surface.

2. Apply the base coat to the surface; let dry. Be careful not to press too hard to avoid flattening the embossed surface.

3. Mix 4 parts glaze to 1 part top coat paint.

4. Apply the glaze/paint mixture to an approximate 3-foot vertical section of the wallpaper. Quickly use the squeegee to drag through the glaze/paint mixture, starting at the top and working your way down. Clean off the squeegee after each pass with the lint-free cloth to remove excess glaze.

5. Continue applying the glaze/paint mixture to the wallpaper, removing some of the mixture with the squeegee until each wall is complete. (Photo A)

PROTECTING SURFACES

■ Because you are squeegeeing paint off a vertical surface, this technique is quite messy. To catch any runoff, tape plastic drop cloths to the molding and floor for protection.

DECOUPAGE

DECOUPAGE—THE CENTURIES-OLD EUROPEAN ART OF CUTTING PAPERS AND APPLYING THEM TO A PROJECT SURFACE with a special decoupage adhesive—isn't a true paint technique, but it is a great way to add color, pattern, and style to a wall, furnishings, or home decorating accessories without hand painting, stenciling, or stamping. Paint can come into play: If the decoupage motifs won't cover an entire project surface, you must select a base coat that will provide a suitable backdrop for the papers. This base coat can be a flat color or you can incorporate any of the techniques featured in this book,

including crackling or colorwashing. If you want a truly unique look, cover the completed decoupaged project with a glaze/paint mixture for additional color and depth.

Special decoupage papers in a wide range of motifs are readily available at crafts and art supply stores as well as on the Internet, but you can also use wallpaper, wrapping paper, greeting cards, scrapbooking papers, reproduction prints, or other heavier papers for this technique. Do not attempt to use magazine or newspaper cutouts: They are too thin, and the printing on the reverse side of the images will bleed through as you apply the decoupage medium.

Vintage botanical prints uniformly decoupaged to the walls of this dressing room add interest without being too fussy.

sideboard style

▲ Decoupage papers in a classy blue and white Italian tile motif cover portions of this clean-line sideboard. Prior to applying the cut paper to the surface, the sideboard is painted with cream and light green paints that stand out against the vivid blue wall.

glazed over

▲ Cozy and dramatic, this powder room combines decoupaged prints with glazed walls. The prints are tea-stained for an instant aged look before being applied to the wall. A protective coat of clear polyurethane is applied over the decoupaged motifs. The walls have five layers of glaze, starting with pink and ending with deep magenta. See page 28 for more information on layering glazes.

exotic decoupage

◄ While rich paint colors—saffron yellow, lotus magenta, and mandarin orange—magnify the mysterious mood of this bedroom, it's the exotic decoupaged images that surprise the eyes. Before being applied to the walls the Indian-influenced images are sprayed with a matte-finish spray formulated for paper products, then painted with a mixture of paint and water of varying intensities. After the images are applied to the wall, a mixture of equal parts sienna glaze and water is painted over all of the images, followed by an application of a gel medium to secure the edges and preserve the papers. The magenta wall above the decoupaged papers features the ragging off technique. See page 64 or more information on ragging off. ▼

decoupage in black and white

▲ This bathroom evokes the charm of a 19th-century English print room: Genteel silhouettes hand-painted on paper and ornate borders and delicate wreaths of paper are decoupaged to the wall.

the **DECOUPAGE** technique

■ Decoupage is really a simple technique—you cut out the desired images and adhere them to a surface—but skill is required for the cutting of the papers. It is most often recommended that you use a small pair of very sharp scissors to cut out decoupage motifs; hold the scissors at an angle close to the edge of the motif as you cut and turn the paper as you cut so that you get a clean edge. If desired you can use a crafts knife and a self-healing cutting mat. After the motifs are adhered to the project surface, you can cover the surface with a glaze/paint mixture in the desired ratio to add another dimension to the project.

YOU WILL NEED

☐ Latex paint for base coat in desired color and finish

☐ Decoupage paper, wallpaper, or other desired paper

☐ Decoupage medium

☐ Scissors or crafts knife and cutting mat

☐ Paintbrushes or foam brushes

☐ Optional: Sponge

☐ Optional: Wallpaper brush

HOW-TO steps

1. Apply the base coat to the surface; let dry.

2. Cut the desired motifs from the paper.

3. Using a paintbrush or foam brush, apply decoupage medium to the back of each motif and adhere the motifs to the project surface in the desired locations. (**Photos A and B**) If excess decoupage medium seeps from beneath the motifs, wipe it away with a damp sponge. If needed use the wallpaper brush to flatten the edges of the papers to ensure they are adhered to the project surface.

4. After all motifs are placed, cover the entire surface with two to three thin, even layers of decoupage medium using a foam brush to seal, allowing the medium to dry between coats.

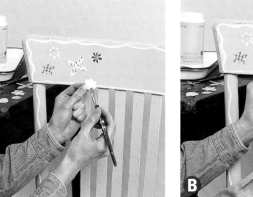
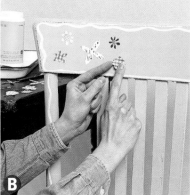

▲ Special decoupage papers similar to these work best for this technique, but you can also use heavier-bodied papers, such as wrapping paper and greeting cards.

TORN PAPER

WHILE APPLYING WALLPAPER TO A WALL OR OTHER SURFACE ISN'T TECHNICALLY A PAINT TREATMENT, adhering randomly torn pieces of patterned wallpaper can emulate the look of a faux finish. If you are using a prepasted wallpaper, follow the manufacturer's directions for application; likewise, if using an unpasted paper, use wallpaper paste to apply per the manufacturer's directions. While you can use a wide variety of papers for this technique, experiment on a sample board before committing to your wall: The colors of some papers may have a tendency to bleed, while others may be too thin and will tear as you apply them.

▲ An arched opening frames a cozy breakfast nook. Pieces of painted orange paper have been torn irregularly and applied to the walls. Where the papers overlap, the white edges are visible, resulting in a striated stone look.

more than **wallpaper**

■ EVERYTHING FROM gift wrap to handmade art papers can be used to liven up nearly every surface in your home, from walls to wood furnishings. In this kitchen small pieces of torn papers are adhered to the wall with wallpaper paste; they serve as a unique collaged backsplash and cornice-look portion of wall above the window. The result is an artful hodgepodge of texture and color that harmonizes with the vivid purple cabinets.

marble-look paper

THIS STYLISH MARBLED WALLPAPER—a combination of white, brown, and gray—has an authentic look of faux finishing when torn and then applied to the walls of this entryway. The hand-torn wallpaper shown is specially formulated for the torn-paper process.

the **TORN PAPER** technique

■ The directions below are for prepasted wallpapers formulated for this purpose. While this prepasted paper is meant to be torn into random shapes and wetted to adhere to the surface, if you use another paper, use a sample board to play with paper positioning and the amount of wallpaper paste needed to ensure the paper will adhere to the wall.

YOU WILL NEED

☐ **Patterned prepasted wallpaper or other desired paper**

☐ **Shallow container with water**

☐ **Wallpaper smoother**

☐ **Optional: Wallpaper paste**

HOW-TO steps

1. Tear the wallpaper or other paper into random pieces. (Photo A)

2. Follow the manufacturer's directions for adhering prepasted wallpaper to the project surface with water; if you are using a different paper, apply wallpaper paste to the back of each piece and apply to the wall. Use the wallpaper smoother to adhere each piece, especially the corners, to the project surface. (Photo B)

3. Continue tearing paper and adhering it to the wall, overlapping the edges, until all surfaces are covered.

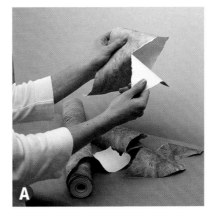
A

B

CREDITS, RESOURCES, and INDEX

CREDITS

Product Credits

Page 34. Base Coat (light blue): Sherwin Williams 6527 Blissful Blue. Top Coat (medium blue): Sherwin Williams 6528 Cosmos. Drapery fabric: Waverly, 666363, Tiny Toile, Sky.

Page 36. Watercolor Walls Colorwash Kit, Spaghetti Squashed.

Page 38. Top Coat: Sherwin Williams Honest Blue 6520. Sofa table: Ethan Allen. Lamp: Jonathan Adler, Ultra Violet Lamp, #JA27. Pottery: Jonathan Adler, Ball, Baby Jane Bud Vase, #JA30; vase to right, Gerard Cylinder Vase, #JA42; tall vase on lower shelf, Viva Vase, #JA29; small vase, Little Joe Bud Vase, #JA31; plate, Half Circles Tray, #JA38; dog dish, Large Dog Bowl, #NOT1. Circle pillow: Jonathan Adler, The Textile Collection. Graphic pillows, 9 Circles. Rug: Jonathan Adler, Sporty 4"x6". Brown pillow: Woolrich. Brown suede fabric: Synergize Fabrics, Kanto Italiano, #9908, Chocolate Brown.

Page 45. Base Coat: Sherwin Williams 7006 Extra White. Top Coat: Laura Ashley Navy 4.

Page 47 (right). Base Coat: Behr 3B59-1 Nature's Tears. Top Coats: Behr 3B59-6 Mountain Grass (High), Behr 3A59-4 Chaparral Pea (Medium), Behr 3A59-3 Smokey Emerald (Low).

Page 47 (left and below). Base Coat: Sherwin Williams 6105 Divine White. Top Coat: Sherwin Williams 6594 Poinsettia. Star hanging hook: World Market.

Page 48. Base Coat: Valspar 347-1 Chowder. Top Coat: Valspar 347-4 Manor Stone. Lamp: Jonathan Adler, Nelson Lamp, #N10W/B. White vases: Jonathan Adler, Gourd #N2W/B. Vase: TAG, Firefly Vase. Rug: Expressions.

Page 49. Base Coat: Valspar 92-42B Bone White. Top Coat: Valspar 268-4 Red Earth.

Page 56. Base Coat: Sherwin Williams 6105 Divine White. Top Coat: Glidden 364 Maple Season. Coffee table: John Greenleaf, Sonoma Area Table, #846W. Rug: Capel, Indian River, #2273, #710 Golden Brown. Rug: By Design. Cashmere throw: Garnet Hill. Leather tacks on coffee table: Turner and Seymour, #N11670421, Pewter Zinc Nails. Wood blinds: Nanik, 2" Wood Blinds, Cognac.

Page 57. Base Coat: Ralph Lauren Barn Red. Top Coat: Ralph Lauren Bankhead Blossom. Panel bed: Woodcraft, Maple Queen Turned-Post Bed, #MCM544. Matlesse: Company Store, Sofia Coverlet, #CG61 and Bed Skirt #GE86, Mocha. Pillow shams: Company Store, Sofia Pillow Shams, #NJ84, Mocha. Blankets and pillows: Woolrich. Rug: Capel, Sausalito, #2280, #300 Ebony. Cashmere throw: Garnet Hill.

Page 58. Top Coat: Dutchboy Tree Moss. Ultrasuede fabric on windows: Synergize Fabrics, #6674 and #6604. Wood blinds: Nanik, 1" Wood Blinds, #118B Frost.

Page 59. Base Coat: Valspar Bone White 92-4B. Top Coat: Behr 3A18-5 Rosin.

Page 61 (top). Base Coat: Sherwin Williams 6536 Searching Blue. Top Coat: Sherwin Williams 6535 Solitude. Rug: Capel, Fireside, #2307, #450 Denim. Drapery fabric: Kravet, Tintorello, 5. Drapery fabric: Robert Allen, Ticking, Natural. Wood blinds: Hunter Douglas, Country Woods Expose Wood Blinds, 102 Golden Bamboo.

Page 61 (bottom). Base Coat: Sherwin Williams 7004 Snowbound. Top Coat: 6198 Sensible Hue. Light fixture: Progress Lighting, P3029-15, Victorian Bath Collection, 3 Light, Polished Chrome. Wall shelf: Umbra, #022655-040, Strand Wall Shelf, Black. Soap dispenser: Umbra, Raya Soap Pump, #020670-040. Wastebasket: Umbra, Raya Waste Can, #082695-040. Cup: Umbra, Raya Tumbler, #020620-040. Magazine rack: Umbra, Trellis Leaning Towel Rack, #020945-213.

Page 63. Base Coat: Valspar 286A-1 Seedling. Top Coat: Valspar 286A-5 Grassy Knoll.

Page 69. Base Coat: Behr 1A35-4. Top Coat: Behr 1B35-2 Mystic Iris.

Page 70 (right). Base Coat: Behr Lucent Sky 1B37-1; Top Coats: Behr 1B40-1 (High); Behr 1B40-2 (Medium); Behr 1A40-4 (Low).

Page 74. Base Coats: Behr Brown Derby, Hazelhurst, and Woodbine. Top Coat: Behr River Sand.

Page 75. Base Coat: Behr 3A15-4 Solomon Sand. Top Coat: Behr 3B15-2 Marble Pedestal.

Page 77. Base Coat: Valspar 347-6 Brown Spar. Top Coat: Valspar 347-3 Weathered Oak. Handles on furniture: Amerock, #1590-WN.

Page 79. Base Coat: Behr 1B16-6 Sun-Dried Orange. Top Coat: Behr 1A16-3 Gingham Peach.

Page 106. Base Coat: Glidden 731 Light Navajo. Top Coat: Sherwin Williams Baize Green (glaze colorwash). Diamonds (applied with brush as colorwash): Glidden 925 Sea Drops; Glidden 930 White Marble; Glidden 1009 Pale Vista; Glidden 1004 Aviary Green; Glidden 1001 Walden's Pond; Sherwin Williams 6429 Baize Green; Sherwin Williams 6428 Honeydew. Carpet: Shaw, Queen Carpet, Style Bradstreet (7G793), Style #Z6028 "Alluring" Color 00112 Champagne, Tuftex by Shaw. Rug: Capel, Seville #2183, Color #600 Cream.

Page 110. Base Coat: Glidden Tailwind 1483. Diamonds: Delta Ceramcoat 02445 Green Sea and Silver Rub 'n Buff. Lamp: Garnet Hill, 1GH8431, Moons of Jupiter Lamp, Blue. Rug: Company Store. Bed skirt: Company Store, Sofia Bed Skirt #GE86, Green. Pillow shams: Company Store, Sofia Pillow Shams, #NJ84, Green. Blue pillowcases: Company Store, Flannel Lace Pillowcases, Mist.

Page 112. Rug: Kid at Heart Designs. Blue bucket: Land of Nod.

Page 114. Base Coat above chair rail: Sherwin Williams Nomadic Desert. Plaid: Sherwin Williams 6109 Hopsack (Dark Brown); 6105 Divine White; 6535 Solitude (Medium Blue); 6536 Searching Blue (Dark Blue); Base Coat below chair rail: Sherwin Williams 6535 Solitude. Drapery fabric: Kravet, Tintorello, 5. Drapery tie fabric: Robert Allen, Ticking, Natural. Chair rail: Georgia Pacific, 3½" chair rail. Wood blinds: Hunter Douglas, Country Woods Expose Wood Blinds, 102, Golden Bamboo.

Page 115. Base Coat loose plaid: Valspar 92-42B Bone White. Plaid: Blue Behr 2B42-2 Gentian Blue; Pink Behr 1A25-4 Open Rose; Orange Laura Ashley Pumpkin 5; Green Valspar 286A-5 Grassy Knoll; Yellow Sherwin Williams Midday 6695. Base Coat multicolor plaid: Behr 2A32-3 Sachet. Plaid: Sherwin Williams Extra White 7006; Red Behr 4C11-1 Knockout Red; Purple Behr 2A36-4 Purple Pop. Base Coat gray plaid: Behr 3B41-2 Minnow. Plaid: Behr 3A41-3 Eaglebend (Darker Gray); Behr 3A51-3 Jack Rabbit (Blue-Gray).

Page 119. Lettering: Painter's Brand Pen, Black. Delta Ceramcoat: Orange: Base Coat: 02433 Island, Top Coat: 02042 Pumpkin; Blue: Base Coat: 02013 Blue Danube. Top Coat: 02038 Ultra Blue; Red: Base Coat: 02084 Lisa Pink. Top Coat: 02053 Bright Red. Yellow: Base Coat: 02064 Sunbright Yellow. Top Coat: 02504 Yellow; Purple: Base Coat: 02456 Dusty Plum. Top Coat: 02577 Deep Lilac; Green: Base Coat: 02072 Lima Green. Top Coat: 02517 Spring Green. Dresser: Woodcraft, Maple Shaker Mule Chest, #CCM511. Jewelry box: Woodcraft, Maple 2-Drawer Jewelry Box, #CCM525. Mirror: Maple Shaker Mirror, #CCM521. Rug: Capel. Rug: Kid at Heart Designs.

Page 120 (right). Base Coat lower wall: Sherwin Williams 6535 Solitude. Base Coat upper 12" portion: Sherwin Williams 6107 Nomadic Desert; Writing Sherwin Williams Bravado Red. Roman shade fabric: Robert Allen, Ticking, Sky. Jute webbing: Wrights, #1839009029. White dishes/blue stemware: World Market. Hardware on corner cabinets: Amerock, #24019-AN.

Page 126. Base Coat: Valspar Spring Breeze. Top Coat: Valspar Paradise Lost; Black. Details: Painter's Brand Pen, Black; Fish picture: Delta Ceramcoat; Background: 02004 Luscious Lemon; Frame 02459 Crocus Yellow; Starfish: Delta Ceramcoat 02459 Crocus Yellow. Monogrammed towels: Garnet Hill, #1GH8099, Krayon Cotton Towels, Yellow. Yellow bucket: Land of Nod.

Page 130 (top). Base Coat lower wall: Sherwin Williams 6674 Jonquil; Base Coat upper wall: Sherwin Williams 7005 Pure

White. Stripes: Sherwin Williams 6674 Jonquil. Base Coat bathtub: Sherwin Williams 6528 Cosmos. Stamping: Delta Ceramcoat 02505 White; 02478 Periwinkle Blue; 02009 Seminole Green; 02502 Pthalo Blue; 02552 Moroccan Red. Light fixture: Progress Lighting, #P3029-06, Victorian Bath Collection, 3 Light, Pearl Nickel. Faucet: Kohler. Bath fixture: Sign of the Crab #P0402M, P0342M, P0007EM, Matte Nickel Finish. Rugs: Colonial Mills. Fabrics: Robert Allen, Ticking, #8530-101, Red. Monogrammed towels and slippers: Garnet Hill, #1GH8099, Krayon Cotton Towels, Yellow.

Page 130 (bottom). Base Coat: Sherwin Williams 6674 Jonquil. Top Coat: Delta Ceramcoat White 02505; Periwinkle Blue 02478; Seminole Green 02009; Pthalo Blue 02502; Moroccan Red 02552.

Page 131. Base Coat: Sherwin Williams 7006 Extra White. Top Coat: Sherwin Williams 6716 Dancing Green. Stamping: Delta Ceramcoat 02508 Opaque Blue. Stamp: Rubber Stampede, Flower Power, 72098. Flooring: Armstrong, Excelon Tile, #51862 Blue Eyes, #51933 Blue Cloud, #51820 Marina Blue. Ceiling fan: Hunter Fan Co., #20436, 42" 5-Blade Beacon Hill, White. Blue pendant light kit: Tiella, #800PND1BLN, Blue Cone Pendant Light Kit. Canister and linens: World Market. Faucet: Kohler, K-7825-K/K-16050-5, Finesse Kitchen Sink Faucet with Swing Spout, Brushed Nickel.

Page 133. Base Coat: Ralph Lauren TH42 Stadium Red. Delta Ceramcoat Seashell White 02541. Duncan Chunky Stamp 18615 Garden Rosebud.

Page 139 (top). Base Coat: Behr 3A59-3 Smokey Emerald; Base Coat chair rail: Sherwin Williams 6694 Glad Yellow. Top Coat lower wall: Sherwin Williams 6451 Nature Green. Stencil border: DécorQuik, Butterflies, 30133.

Page 145. Stencil: Da Buzz, Petite Repeats by Jan Dressler.

Page 147. Base Coat wall and mantel trim: TruValue E-Z Kare Red Rivers; Base Coat mantel: TruValue E-Z Kare Sandy Bay. Top Coat marble: Delta Ceramcoat 02435 Trail Tan; Veining: Delta Ceramcoat 02077 Cardinal Red; 02506 Black. Lamp: Artemide, Style #009048, Tizio Classic Lamp, Black. Rug: Capel, Lyric-Camel, #8060, #850 Terra Cotta. Animal statues, balls, journal, candle: World Market. Blanket: Woolrich.

Page 148. Stripes: Sherwin Williams 6428 Honeydew and Sherwin Williams 6429 Baize Green. Base Coat below chair rail: Sherwin Williams 6429 Baize Green. Base Coat marble: Glaze Glidden 731 Light Navajo. Top Coat marble: Glaze Glidden 925 Sea Drops; Veining Delta Ceramcoat 02025 Burnt Umber. Carpet: Queen carpet, Style Bradstreet (7G793), Style #Z6028 "Alluring" Color 00112 Champagne, Tuftex by Shaw.

Page 149. Base Coat: Behr 3A41-3 Eaglebend. Top Coat:

Sherwin Williams 7006 Extra White. Black Veining: Delta Ceramcoat 02056 Black.

Page 157. Base Coat walls: Glidden #2012 Swiss Coffee; Base Coat yellow cabinets: Ralph Lauren Yellowhammer; Base Coat red cabinets: Ralph Lauren Barn Red. Toile wallpaper: Waverly, Classics Lifestyles, #564300. Toile fabric: Waverly, Classic Lifestyles book, Country Life fabric, #659430. Countertop: Wilsonart, Manitoba Maple, #7911-60. Faucet: Kohler, #K-690, Vinnata Kitchen Sink Faucet with Pull-Down Spray, Brushed Nickel. Hardware: Amerock, #BP9365-G10 Bin Pulls; #BP1586-G10 Knobs. Woven shade: Hunter Douglas, Tahiti, Straw Hut #WWTA245A96F. Appliances: G.E.

Page 158. Base Coat beaded board and upper wall: Glidden #423 Worsted Tan. Top Coat beaded board: Glidden #560 Russian White. Light fixture: Progress Lighting, #P3028-74, Victorian Bath Collection, 2 Light, Venetian Bronze. Faucet: Delta, Victorian Collection #2555-RBLHP, Centerset Faucet, Venetian Bronze. Paneling: Georgia Pacific, Ply-Bead Real Wood Panels.

Page 160. Top Coat: TruValue E-Z Kare Classic Red.

Page 163. Base Coat: Behr 1A42-3 Big Sky. Top Coat: Behr 1A14-3 Cut Squash.

Page 165. Base Coat (walls and glaze wash on bed): Glidden Pinwheel; Scallped Edge: Glidden Pinwheel glaze with Delta Ceramcoat; Ladybugs: Delta Ceramcoat 02056 Berry Red. Details: Painter's Brand Pen, Black; Whitewash: 2/3 Sherwin Williams Extra White, 1/3 water. Headboard: Mastercraft, #1938, Twin Beaded-Board Headboard. Paneling: Georgia Pacific, Unfinished Ply-Bead Board. Eyelet bed skirt: Company Store, Twin Eyelet Bed Skirt, #GE93. Curtain fabric: Robert Allen, Twirling, Pastel. Rug: Garnet Hill, #GH0972, 3x5, Chenille Braided Rug. Pink metal bin: Land of Nod, #1005051-PI, Pink Holy Storage Bins.

Page 168. Base Coat upper wall: Sherwin Williams 6179 Artichoke. Top Coat (top portion upper wall): Sherwin Williams 6178 Clary Sage. Base Coat lower wall: Sherwin Williams 6178 Clary Sage. Top Coat lower wall: Sherwin Williams 6175 Sagey. Horizontal Stripe: Sherwin Williams 6176 Livable Green.

Page 173. Wallpaper: Wall White, Imperial Home Décor Group. Sideboard: Ethan Allen, 28-6206-282, Horizons Buffett. Prints on wall: By Design. Lamp: By Design.

Page 177. Base Coat: Sherwin Williams 6715 Lime Granite. Top Coat: Behr 3A59-4 Chaparral Pea.

Page 179. Base Coats: Delta Ceramcoat 02523 Butter Cream; 02447 Village Green. Paper: Papers by Catherine, Rossi Italian Print, Blue Tile. Sideboard: John Greenleaf, Shaker Huntboard, #472W. Hardware: Amerock Guardian Accentz, BP9338-G10 and BP9365-G10. Lamp: Garnet Hill, 1GH8431, Moons of Jupiter Lamp, Blue.

Page 186. Wallpaper: Village PaperIllusion Color Multi #5805265. Hardware: Amerock, #BP1586-G10, Knobs.

Photography, Styling, and Painting Credits

PHOTOGRAPHY

Photography, Fran Brennan: Pages 32–33.

Photography, RossChapple: Page 53.

Photography, Kent Clawson: Pages 17–19, 20 (bottom), 21, 34, 36–38, 41, 45, 47–49, 56–59, 61, 63, 65 (bottom), 69, 70 (right), 72 (bottom), 74–77, 79, 88–89, 106, 110, 112, 114–115, 119 (top), 120 (right), 121 (bottom), 126–127, 129 (bottom), 130–131, 133, 135, 137, 139 (top), 145, 147–149, 153, 157–160, 163, 165, 167–168, 171–173, 177, 179, 183, 186–187, 194–208.

Photography, Cheryl Dalton: Page 122.

Photography, Bob Greenspan: Page 139 (bottom).

Photography, Jamie Hadley: Page 146.

Photography, Emily Minton: Page 98.

Additional photography courtesy of the following

Meredith publications: *Better Homes and Gardens®magazine, Better Homes and Gardens® Do It Yourselfmagazine, Better Homes and Gardens® Bedroom & Bathmagazine, Better Homes and Gardens® Decoratingmagazine, Better Homes and Gardens® Kids' Roomsmagazine, Better Homes and Gardens® Paint Decor magazine, Better Homes and Gardens® Quick & Easy Decorating magazine, Better Homes and Gardens® Simply Perfect Walls magazine, Better Homes and Gardens® Window & Wall Ideas magazine, Traditional Home® Decorator Showhousemagazine.*

STYLING

Styling, Susan Andrews: Page 139 (bottom).

Styling, Brian Carter: Page 98.

Styling, Cheryl Dalton: Page 122.

Styling, Carla Howard: Page 146.

Styling, Cathy Kramer, Cathy Kramer Designs: Pages 34, 36, 38, 47–48, 56–58, 61, 74, 77, 106, 110, 112, 114, 119 (top)), 120 (right), 126, 130–131, 147–148, 157–158, 160, 165, 168, 173, 179, 186.

Styling, Linda Krinn: Page 53.

Styling, Joetta Moulden: Pages 32–33.

PAINTING

Painting, Tina Blanck: Page 139 (bottom).

Painting, Peggy DelRosario: Page 146.

Painting, Patty Mohr Kramer: Pages 34, 38, 47–48, 56–57, 61, 77, 106, 110, 114, 119 (top), 120 (right), 126, 130–131, 139 (top), 147–148, 157–158, 165, 168, 173, 179.

Painting, Amy Queen: Pages 32–33.

Painting, Amy Tincher-Durik: Pages 36, 147, 160.

RESOURCES

BORDERS, ETC.

Caldwell Design
888/422-6685
www.wallwords.com
Vinyl letter and phrase rub-ons.

Decal Specialties
610/644-9200
www.decalspecialties.com
Hand-painted look borders, rub-ons, decals.

DECOUPAGE SUPPLIES

The Adhesive Products, Inc.
510/526-7616
www.crafterspick.com
Decoupage medium.

Artifacts, Craft Division
903/729-4178
www.maryjeanonline.com
Decoupage papers.

Papers by Catherine
713/723-3334
www.papersbycatherine.com
Decoupage papers.

FLOORCLOTH CANVAS

Kunin Felt, Foss Manufacturing Company
800/292-7900
www.kuninfelt.com
Preprimed canvas in roll or precut shapes.

GENERAL SUPPLIES

American Traditional Stencils
800/448/6656
www.americantraditional.com
Laser-cut stencils, stencil-look rub-on borders, stenciling accessories, foam stamps.

DecoArt
800/367-3047
www.decoart.com
Acrylic and stenciling paints, crackle medium, specialty paint finishes.

Delta Technical Coatings
800/423-4135
www.deltacrafts.com
Acrylic paints, stencils, stenciling brushes and adhesives, foam stamps.

Duncan Enterprises
800/438/6266
www.duncancrafts.com
Acrylic paints, decoupage medium foam stamps.

Plaid Enterprises
678/291-8100
www.plaidonline.com
Laser-cut and border stencils, foam stamps, stencil and specialty brushes, acrylic and enamel paints, glazes, decoupage medium, specialty paint tools and accessories.

PAINT

Behr
800/854-0133
www.behr.com
Primer, latex and alkyd paint, glaze.

Benjamin Moore
800/672-4686
www.benjaminmoore.com
Primer, latex and alkyd paint, glaze.

Glidden and ICI Paints Brand
800/GLIDDEN (454-3336)
www.glidden.com
Primer, latex and alkyd paint, glaze.

Kling Magnetics
800/523-9640
www.kling.com
Magnetic paint.

Krylon Products Group
800/832-2541
www.krylon.com
Primer, spray, chalkboard, plastic, glow-in-the-dark and other specialty paints and finishes, paint pens.

Ralph Lauren
800/379-POLO (7656)
www.polo.com
Latex paints, specialty finishes, glazes, accessories.

Rust-Oleum Corporation
800/553-8444
www.rust-oleum.com
Primer, spray and other specialty paints and finishes.

Sherwin Williams
800/474-3794
www.sherwin-williams.com
Primer, latex and alkyd paint, glaze, specialty paint tools and accessories.

SkimStone
800/444-7833
www.skimstone.com
Interior concrete paint.

Tru-Test
773/695-5000
www.truevalue.com
Primer, latex and alkyd paint, specialty paint tools and accessories.

Valspar
888/313-5569
www.valspar.com
Primer, latex and alkyd paint, glaze, crackle medium, specialty paint tools and accessories..

Watercolor Walls Colorwash
866/302-6567
www.watercolorwalls.com
Colorwash kits, coordinating stencils.

PAINTBRUSHES AND OTHER TOOLS

Royal and Langnickel Brush Manufacturing
800/247-2211
www.royalbrush.com
Natural and synthetic bristle brushes, artist's brushes, sea sponges, check rollers, combs, specialty brushes.

World Wide Distribution Associates
973/208-6937
www.wwda.com
WallMagic Decorative Painting Kit (double roller).

PROJECTORS

Artograph
888/975-9555
www.artograph.com
Projectors for various uses.

STAMPS

Rubber Stampede
800/632-8386
www.rubberstampede.com
Foam stamps.

STENCILS

Dressler Stencil Company, Jan Dressler Stencils
888/656-4515
www.dresslerstencils.com
Laser-cut stencils and stenciling accessories.

Stencil Ease
800/334-1776
www.stencilease.com
Laser-cut stencils and stenciling accessories.

StenSource International
800/642-9293
www.stensource.com
Stencils and stenciling accessories.

WALLPAPER

FSC Wallcoverings
212/213-7900
www.villagehome.com
PaperIllusion product designed for torn paper technique.

Imperial Home Decor Group
www.ihdg.com
Anaglypta embossed wallpaper.

OTHER PRODUCTS FEATURED IN THIS BOOK

Amerock Corporation
800/618-9559
www.amerock.com
Cabinetry hardware and accessories.

Artemide
631/694-9292
www.artemide.com
Light fixtures.

Capel
800/320-7847
www.capelrugs.com
Rugs.

Clawfoot Supply
877/682-4192
www.clawfootsupply.com
Faucets, tubs, plumbing, other bath accessories.

The Company Store
800/285-3696
www.thecompanystore.com
Bedding, down bedding, furnishings, decorative accessories.

Delta
800/345-DELTA (33582)
www.deltafaucet.com
Faucets, handles, bath accessories.

Garnet Hill
800/622.6216
www.garnethill.com
Bedding, furnishings, decorative accessories.

GE Consumer Products
800/626-2000
www.geappliances.com
Appliances.

Georgia-Pacific Corp.
800/BUILDGP (2845347)
www.gp.com
Wood panels, plywood, lumber, gypsum board, molding.

Hunter Douglas
800/937-STYLE (77895)
www.hunterdouglas.com
Blinds, shades.

Jonathan Adler
877/287-1910
www.jonathanadler.com
Pottery, lamps, furnishings, textiles, decorative accessories.

Kid At Heart Designs
214/361-5177
www.kidatheartdesigns.com
Rugs.

Kohler Co.
800/456-4537
www.kohler.com
Sinks, tubs, faucets, furnishings, decorative accessories.

Master Craft
800/327-0890
email: mastercraftfurniture@hotmail.com
Furnishings.

Nanik
800/422-4544
www.springs.com
Blinds.

Progress Lighting
864/599-6000
www.progresslighting.com
Light fixtures.

The Robert Allen Group
800/240-8189
www.robertallendesign.com
Fabric, trims, drapery hardware.

Shaw Carpets
800/441-7429
www.shawfloors.com
Carpeting, area rugs, ceramic, hardwood, and laminate flooring.

Synergized Fabrics, Inc.
617/889-4150
Fabric. For cut yardage contact United Fabrics, Inc., 856/665-2040

tag
800/621-8350
www.tagltd.com
Decorative accessories.

tiella
847/410-4400
www.tiella.com or www.techlighting.com
Light fixtures.

Turner and Seymour
800/733-9214
www.turnerseymour.com
Upholstery nails.

Umbra
800-387-5122
www.umbra.com
Furnishings, decorative accessories, cabinetry hardware.

Waverly
800/423-5881
www.waverly.com
Fabric, wallcoverings, furnishings, decorative accessories.

William E. Wrights
www.wrights.com
Ribbons, trims, embellishments

Wilsonart International
800/433-3222
www.wilsonart.com
Laminate flooring.

Woodcraft Industries
814/355-5000
www.woodcraftindustries.com
Unfinished furnishings.

Woolrich, Inc.
877/512-7305
www.woolrich.com
Blankets, throws, decorative accessories.

World Market
www.costplusworldmarket.com
Furnishings, decorative accessories.

INDEX

INDEX *continued*

DO YOU LOVE THE EXCITING LOOK OF CRACKLE or are you dreaming about how your kitchen cabinets would look with a distressed paint finish but you aren't sure where to begin? This exciting glossary contains full-size swatches of 15 techniques in various color combinations, which you can tear out of this book and hold up to your project surface to better envision how the finished treatment will look. In addition, the top and base coat paint colors are provided. Note that for the techniques featured on pages 194–203 that the top coat paint has been mixed with glaze in a 1 part paint to 4 parts glaze ratio.

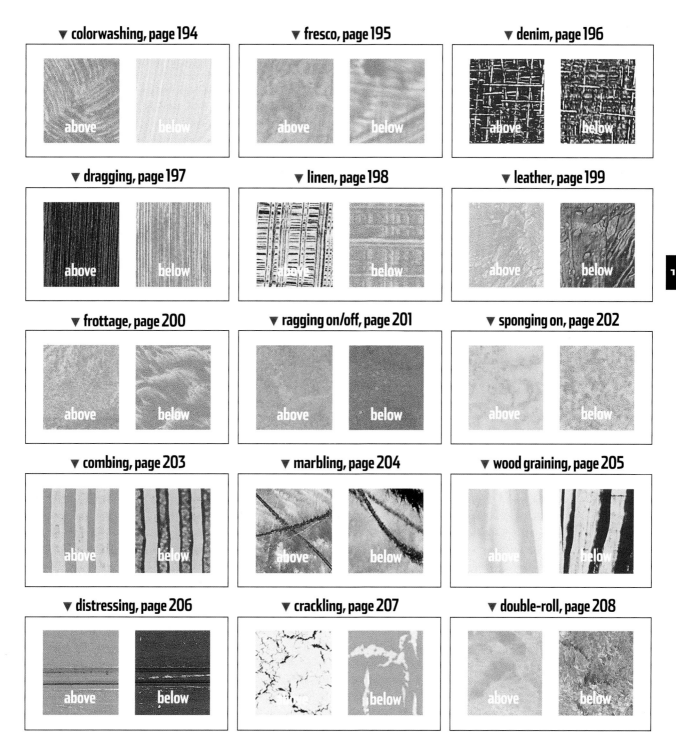

▼ colorwashing, page 194

▼ fresco, page 195

▼ denim, page 196

▼ dragging, page 197

▼ linen, page 198

▼ leather, page 199

▼ frottage, page 200

▼ ragging on/off, page 201

▼ sponging on, page 202

▼ combing, page 203

▼ marbling, page 204

▼ wood graining, page 205

▼ distressing, page 206

▼ crackling, page 207

▼ double-roll, page 208

193

▲ **colorwashing** (above): **BASE COAT** Valspar 91-45A Seltzer Water; **TOP COAT** Glidden Versailles

colorwashing (below): **BASE COAT** Sherwin Willaims 6371 Vanillin; **TOP COAT** Sherwin Williams 6347 Torchlight ▼

▲ **fresco** (above): **BASE COAT** Sherwin Williams 6717 Lime Rickey; **TOP COAT** Sherwin Williams 6400 Lucent Yellow

fresco (below): **BASE COAT** Valspar 91-45A Seltzer Water; **TOP COAT** Behr 1A41-3 Palace Blue ▼

▲ **denim** (above): **BASE COAT** Valspar 91-45A Seltzer Water; **TOP COAT** Valspar 95-7C Mary Mac Red

denim (below): **BASE COAT** Valspar 91-45A Seltzer Water; **TOP COAT** Valspar 9-28C Welcoming Blue ▼

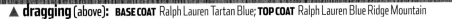

▲ **dragging** (above): **BASE COAT** Ralph Lauren Tartan Blue; **TOP COAT** Ralph Lauren Blue Ridge Mountain

dragging (below): **BASE COAT** Behr 3B21-2 Vintage Rose; **TOP COAT** Behr 3A21-5 Powdered Nutmeg ▼

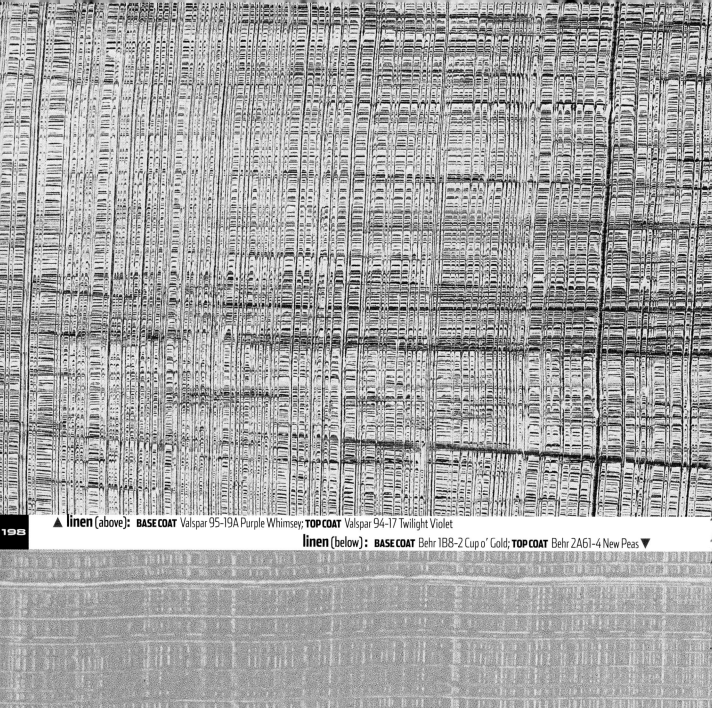

▲ **linen** (above): **BASE COAT** Valspar 95-19A Purple Whimsey; **TOP COAT** Valspar 94-17 Twilight Violet

linen (below): **BASE COAT** Behr 1B8-2 Cup o' Gold; **TOP COAT** Behr 2A61-4 New Peas ▼

▲ **leather** (above): **BASE COAT** Sherwin Williams 6694 Glad Yellow; **TOP COAT** Sherwin Williams 6685 Trinket

leather (below): **BASE COAT** Behr 3B51-2 Kestrel Blue; **TOP COAT** Behr 3A45-5 Antique Pewter ▼

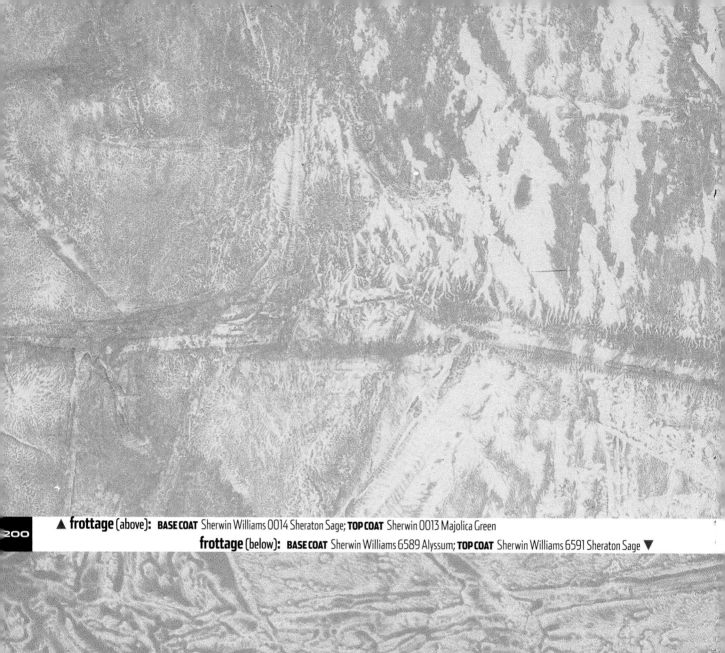

▲ **frottage** (above): **BASE COAT** Sherwin Williams 0014 Sheraton Sage; **TOP COAT** Sherwin 0013 Majolica Green

frottage (below): **BASE COAT** Sherwin Williams 6589 Alyssum; **TOP COAT** Sherwin Williams 6591 Sheraton Sage ▼

▲ **ragging on** (above): **BASE COAT** Sherwin Williams 0004 Rose Brocade; **TOP COAT** (no glaze) Sherwin Williams 0001 Mulberry Silk

ragging off (below): **BASE COAT** Valspar 95-7C Mary Mac Rae; **TOP COAT** Valspar 95-19A Purple Whimsey ▼

▲ **sponging on** (above): **BASE COAT** Glidden Fresh Lime; **TOP COAT #1** Glidden Lime Twist ; **TOP COAT #2** Behr 2B59-1 Fern Tint

sponging on (below): **BASE COAT** Glidden Versailles; **TOP COAT #1** Glidden Pearl Violet; **TOP COAT #2** Sherwin Williams 6815 Awesome Violet ▼

▲ **combing** (above): **BASE COAT** Behr 2A49-3 Saratoga; **TOP COAT** Behr 2B48-1 O'Hara Diamond

combing (below): **BASE COAT** Glidden Pearle Violet; **TOP COAT** Ralph Lauren Oxfordshire ▼

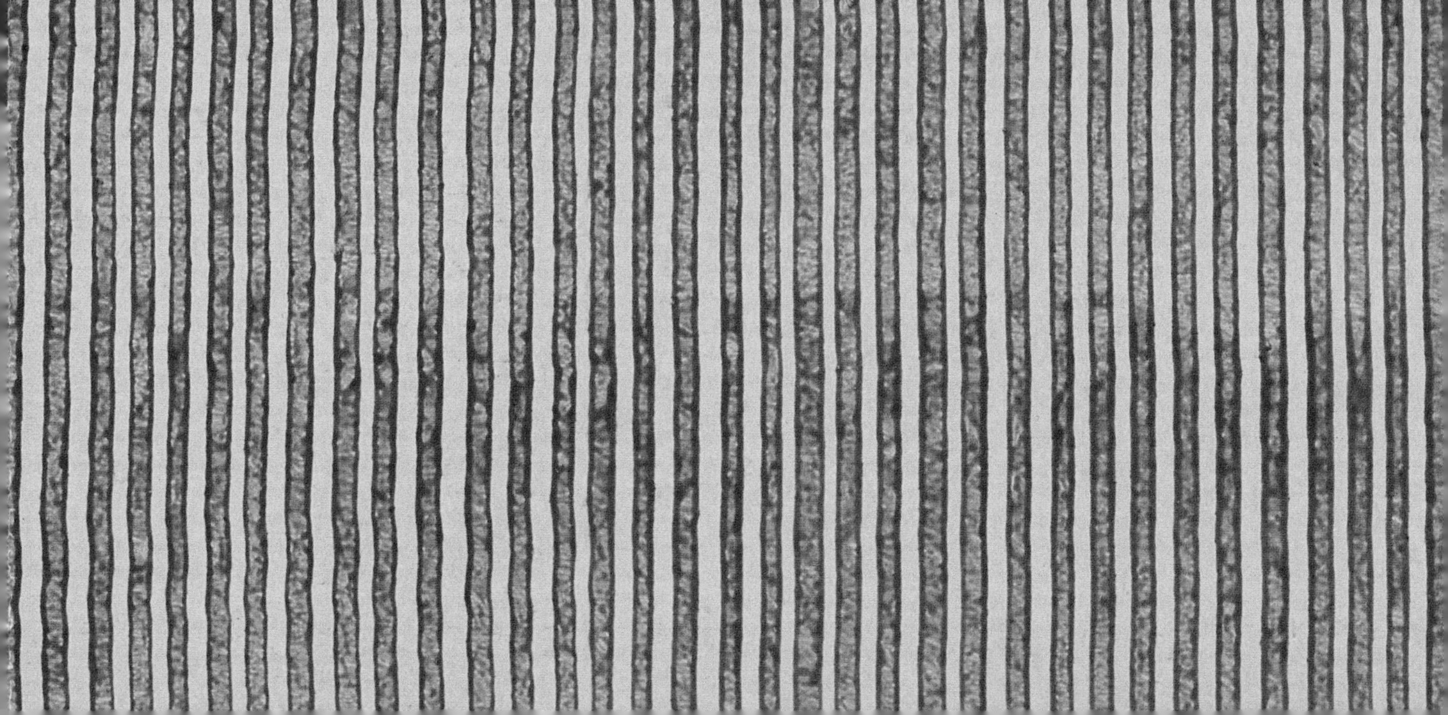

▲ **marbling** (above): **BASE COAT** Valspar 91-45A Seltzer Water; **TOP COAT** Ralph Lauren Blue Ridge Mountain; **VEINING** Delta Ceramcoat 02413 Prussian Blue

marbling (below): **BASE COAT** Glidden Pearl Violet; **TOP COAT** Delta Ceramcoat 02543 Rain Grey; **VEINING** Delta Ceramcoat 02116 Black Green ▼

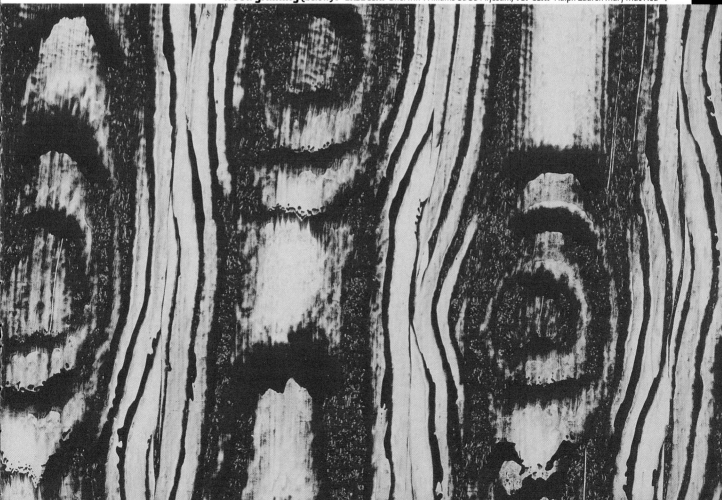

▲ **wood graining** (above)**:** **BASE and TOP COAT** Behr Green Caper 2A59-4

wood graining (below)**:** **BASE COAT** Sherwin Williams 6589 Alyssum; **TOP COAT** Ralph Lauren Mary Mac Red ▼

▲ **distressing** (above): **BASE COAT** Behr 1B16-6 Sun-Dried Orange; **TOP COAT** Behr 2A1-4 Salted Ash

distressing (below): **BASE COAT** Behr 4C11-1 Knockout Red; **TOP COAT** Valspar 277-5 Capitol ▼

▲ **crackling** (above with sponge): **BASE COAT** Valspar 95-19A Purple Whimsey; **TOP COAT** Behr 2A61-4 New Peas

crackling (below with brush): **BASE COAT** Valspar 92-42B Bone White; **TOP COAT** Behr 2A1-4 Salted Ash ▼

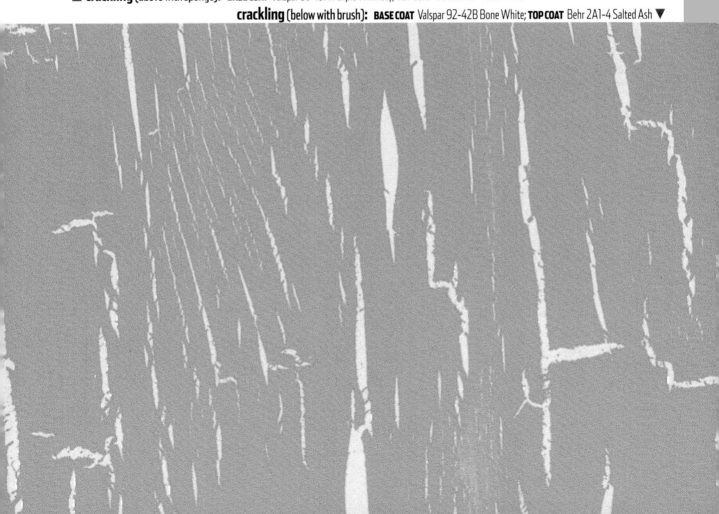

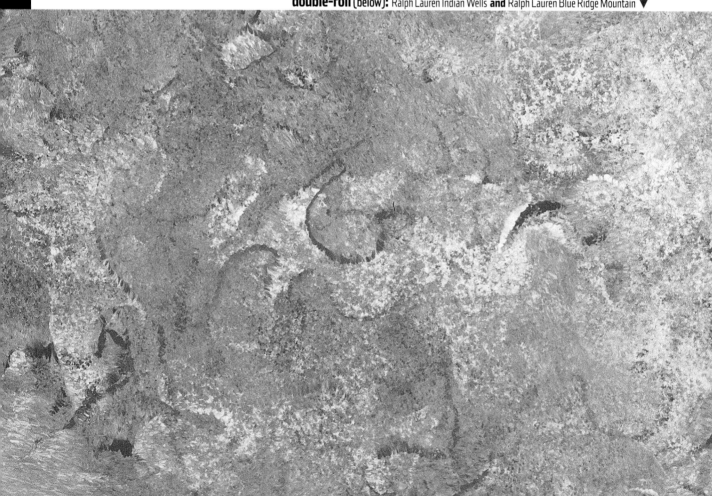

▲ **double-roll** (above): Sherwin Williams 0001 Mulberry Silk **and** Sherwin Williams 6065 Bona Fide Beige

double-roll (below): Ralph Lauren Indian Wells **and** Ralph Lauren Blue Ridge Mountain ▼